THE PROPHETS
OF
ISLAM

Biographical Sketches
according to al Qur'an

PUBLISHED BY
ALHUDA FOUNDATION, INC.

Published by
ALHUDA FOUNDATION, INC.
35 West Demarest Avenue
Englewood, NJ 07631

First USA Edition 1994
Library of Congress Number : 94-070868
ISBN : 1-885140-00-2

Distributors

SHAMSi ENTERPRISES, INC.
35 West Demarest Avenue
Englewood, NJ 07631
Telephone: (201) 569-8123
FAX   : (201) 871-1927

"Seek knowldge from the cradle to the grave."
Prophet Muhammad

THE PROPHETS
OF
ISLAM

Biographical Sketches
according to al Qur'an

Written by
SYED MUHAMMAD HUSSAIN SHAMSI
Nairobi, Kenya

First Printing in Urdu
under the auspices of
Sayyeda Begum
Mumtaz Manzil, Narowal
PAKISTAN

First English Translation by
SYED HAIDER HUSSAIN SHAMSI
Demarest, NJ 07627

CONTENTS

Dedications

This book is dedicated primarily to the seekers of Truth, to the Youth of Islam, and to the New Muslims who have adopted the Straight Path to ensure their salvation.

The translation of this book is dedicated to my late mother who salvaged the Manuscript from the closet and had it published in the Urdu language.

Syed Haider H. Shamsi, M.D.

Acknowledgments

I must thank my wife Dr. Adiba K. Shamsi for her total support in my efforts to translate this book. She cheerfully put up with my late hours at the home computer after her long and strenuous day at work. She read the translated manuscript for errors of typography and syntax, so that the readers of this book may enjoy it without the annoying interruptions.

I also thank Br. Nasir Shamsi for carefully screening the contents of the translation for their accuracy and authenticity. His scholarly knowledge of the religious literature has been fully utilized in the preparation of the English book.

Br. Aunali Khalfan gave me valuable technical advice and suggestions for the layout and the final shape of this book. I thank him for his time and assistance.

Syed Haider H. Shamsi, M.D.

Syed Muhammad Hussain Shamsi
(1878-1962)

ABOUT THE AUTHOR

Syed Muhammad Hussain Shamsi was born on December 24, 1878 at Narowal, District Sialkot, British India. He lost his father at an early age. Even at a young and tender age, he started to work to help his mother and younger sibs. He left home for the tiny State of Jammu for education, about thirty miles north of Narowal. He was a brilliant student of the oriental languages, English and Biblical Studies. He scored the second highest position in Biblical Studies in the Panjab University examination for the entire region.

He had a passion for the healing sciences, but the mundane need for survival took its priority. After matriculation, destiny took him to the newly opened territory of Kenya. He enrolled to work for the British Railways in Kenya. Here he found himself to be one of the few educated people. He saw a unique opportunity to serve a nascent Muslim Community in a strange new land. He led the ritual prayers for them, attended to their funerals, weddings and answered their questions on Islamic Fiqh related to their daily lives. He led and participated in several interfaith debates and dialogues about Islam. All this essentially stimulated him to remain up-to-date in Islamic and other non- Islamic literature. In so doing, he built up a large personal library of reference books which people borrowed to read on their own.

He was committed to education, propagation and the defence of his faith. Towards this end, he started evening and week end schools for the young and the adults, and initially used his own premises for most activities.

As the community enlarged, he participated actively to build the first mosque in Nairobi, and to employ an *alim* (a Muslim minister and a jurist) to carry out the daily religious practices. However he continued his services at a personal level throughout his life.

He died in Mayo Hospital, Lahore on October 18, 1962 attended by his youngest son who was a medical student at that time. His passion came to fruition. He saw his son in the Medical School and in his service by his bed side.
He was buried besides his father in their family cemetary at Narowal, Pakistan.

A HUMBLE REQUEST FROM THE READER

Dear Brother/Sister in Islam,

Please pray for my parents and grand parents, as well as for my husband Syed Muhammad Hussain Shamsi, the author of this book and his parents, and recite the *Sura Fateha* for their eternal benefit. May *Allah* protect you from evil and bless you with health and prosperity in this world, and make available means for your salvation in the hereafter. May *Muhammad wa Ale Muhammad* shower you with peace and tranquility in this world and the next, *Amin.*

Sayyeda Begum
Mumtaz Manzil
Narowal, Pakistan
1980

AUTHOR'S FOREWORD

It was generally felt that whereas there is a lot of written material available on the lives of the Prophets, the beginners, especially the young students are unable to benefit from these voluminous works. This problem became more obvious when I was teaching at Sunday School on Islam to young children of the Nairobi Muslim Community. Although no one is expected to know all the generally quoted number of the prophets of one hundred and twenty four thousand, the children were unfamiliar with even the names of those mentioned in the Qur'an. To fill this gap, it was therefore felt that a brief narrative be compiled about these prophets. This is how this booklet came to be compiled.

The beginning of the book has an abbreviated Table of Genealogy of the Prophets, starting with Adam and concluding with Muhammed. This should provide an historical perspective to these greart personalities. The narratives are purposely kept brief to facilitate memorization and retention.

It is hoped that this book will fulfil the need that was being felt.

With Sincere Wishes
Syed Muhammed Hussain Shamsi
Nairobi, Kenya
November 15, 1956

Translator's Foreword

The present booklet on biographical sketches of the Prophets of Islam mentioned in the Qur'an is one of the three books compiled by my late father, when he was teaching Muslim youth at a Sunday School in Nairobi. Initially this consisted of notes and hand outs to the students. Later these materials were organized in the form of books. For many years after his death, these manuscripts remained unpublished. While spending her last days in Pakistan, my late mother took the initiative to have the first of these manusripts published in Urdu language. She wished that the years of research and experience invested in these books should not go waste and the young and new Muslims should continue to benefit from his writings. Unfortunately, she did not live long enough to see the publication of the remaining manuscripts. All copies of the first print in Urdu have been distributed by now, and reprinting of the book is being planned for the continuation of this noble mission.

I most dearly cherish the memories of being associated by my father in the preparation of these teaching materials. I was then a teenager and enjoyed these assignments. I felt happy to carry out the research projects. It is a long time since my youth that I was again given an assignment to teach Muslim youth at a Sunday School in Englewood, New Jersey. This has also gone on for several years now. I felt that the need for educational materials for young children is no different now than it was about half a century ago. This prompted me to embark on translating my father's works from Urdu to the English language.

I have tried to adhere to the style and the spirit of my father's original works. He tried to keep his narratives of all Prophets before Prophet Muhammad within the confines of information provided in the Qur'an. Occasionally he added information from the authentic Islamic traditions. His intention was to avoid confusion arising from controversial traditions, and to make the narratives brief enough for the children to memorize them. He did not quote the exact *ayas* of the Qur'an just to maintain the continuity of the text. He preferred to give references of the relevant *Suras* at the end of each narrative. In doing so, he intended to assist the curious reader towards personal research from the Qur'an.

Islam aims to bring out the best of the human being within an individual by strengthening the personality. The Qur'an is the guide for achieving this goal. It must be understood that the Qur'an as a book is neither an encyclopedia nor a compendium of any singular subject. However, the Qur'anic references cover enormous topics with precision and depth. Every one can get sufficient guidance and benefit from its contents according to his/her intelligence or search. References to the prophets are made at various occasions as necessitated in illustrating a particular character or during the derivation of a lesson or moral conclusion. Qur'an is the only Holy Scripture that uses this unique methodology to teach man about his past and provide guidance for his present and his future.

All prophets were sent by the Creator to guide mankind. Some of them were charged with greater responsibility than the others, and were given the Cannonic code of conduct to be handed down to the people for their guidance. Consequently the references and narrative description of these prophets occurs with greater frequency in various *Suras*. Some prophets are named while others are only mentioned with a reference to an event, or when a lesson or message is intended.

Middle Eastern nations share a common ancestary and they trace their genealogy to the same patriarchs. Two mainstream peoples have been identified in history. One of these people are the Israilites, the children of Prophet Ya'qub (a son of Prophet Ishaq), while the other are the Arabs, the children of Prophet Ismail, the elder brother of Prophet Ishaq. While addressing the Arabs, the Qur'an makes frequent references to Bani Israil, the Jews. The Message of the Qur'an is however universal. Allah has sent prophets to all people wherever they dwell on Earth, and hence the Last Testament of Allah i.e. the Qur'an, brought by The Last Prophet, is intended for all mankind wherever they may dwell on Earth.

The Message of The Last Prophet is the same as that of The First Prophet, and for the entire humankind created by The One and The Only God. It is for this reason that the author of this book found it necessary to provide greater details on the life of the Last Prophet. He was more proximal to our time. The Qur'an proclaimed him to be the Seal of Prophecy. Which means there will be no prophet after him. He lends authenticity to all previous Holy Scriptures and completes the Divine Message for the human race. Allah has called him *"Rahmatun-lil-aalameen"*, the Blessing for the Universe.

I have been fortunate to collaborate my efforts with brother Nasir Shamsi in reading, reviewing and editing the English content of the language and the text. I also sought the help of several youth to read the text and comment on the flow and readability of the narratives. At the suggestions received from most readers, the salutations after the names of prophets, that are traditional in Urdu (Persian and Arabic) language were dropped to ensure easy and uninterrupted reading.

I sincerely hope that this book will find its place in every home with children and be read and memorized as intended by the author. This book will also provide a stimulus to young people to carry out research on their own, frequently referring to the Qur'an and improving their lives through proper understanding of the Divine Message.

Syed Haider H. Shamsi
Demarest, New Jersey,
USA (1994)

Editor's Comments

The genesis of this book lies in the author's abiding interest in the comparative study of the Monotheistic Faiths-Judaism, Christianity and Islam. Having majored in the Biblical Studies, with distintion, he continued to benefit from the wisdom *(Hikma')* of the Revealed Word through regular study of the Qur'an.

A few years ago, Br. Haider Shamsi and myself were teaching the young students in the Sunday School in Englewood, NJ. I was to teach about the Prophets mentioned in the Qur'an and there was no English book available on the subject. When Br. Haider Shamsi told me that his late father had written a book on the Prophets in Urdu language, I knew that we will have its translation available some day.

Br. Haider is man of his word. By the Grace of Allah, he has translated the book in English. I sincerely hope this will meet the need of the young as well as the New Muslims in particular, and students of religion in general. This excellent work will also help the readers to recognize the essential link and commonality of belief in the Oneness of God, the Prophesy and the Day of Judgement among the followers of the three Monotheistic Faiths. May they learn to live in peace, and endeavour to make this world a better and safer place for their children.

Nasir Shamsi
Jackson, NJ
Sunday, February 6, 1994

LISTING OF THE PROPHETS

xiii

ADAM

THE CREATION OF ADAM

The most widely held belief about the origin of Adam has been that Allah created him from non-existence by His Will using the earth materials. This did not involve the biological processes of evolution or reproduction. Allah created Man and Woman from clay in the form and shape, the way they are today. Any belief or controversy to the contrary is only a speculation.

Different peoples in the world have stories concerning the origin of Man, which point towards the spontanious arrival of the patriarch with his family.

The Hindu believe that man's original parents were Mahadev and Parwati and that they looked like human beings, but were the image of Parmishwar (God Himself). The Jews and the Christians also believe that God created Adam in His own image.

Most people believe that God has no physical form, then how could He create Man in His own image!

This riddle was solved by the last Prophet of Islam when he said "Allah had created Adam with His quality, not His form." Allah can be recognised by His qualities alone. So the saying of the Prophet makes it clear that the image of Allah refers to His qualities.

1

The Prophet further said "Adopt the qualities of Allah."

This becomes clear from the Qur'an where Allah says that He created Adam on this earth as His representative. A representative follows orders. Only one who can execute the orders properly can be a true representative or vicegerent, otherwise there would be errors. Thus, according to the Prophet, assuming the responsibilities of a worthy representative requires the acqisition of the conduct of the master. This, then is what is meant by "God created Man in His image."

ADAM, THE CALIPH OF ALLAH

When Allah desired to create Adam He addressed the angels and said that He was going to create Man and appoint him as His representative on earth. As soon as the creation was accomplished and He had bestowed Adam with His spirit, He told them to bow down in obedience to Adam. The angels who considered themselves to be superior to Adam on account of their closeness to the Creator Himself, were surprised at this instruction to bow down in obedience to a creature that was molded from earth materials. They said to Allah, "You are appointing a being as your vicegerent who would bring unrest and blood shed on earth, whereas we, who have been immersed in your worship were more deserving to receive this honor.

Allah said to them that what was known to Him could not be in their knowledge, and that Adam was specifically suited for the position He had designed for the earth. He offered them a chance to compete in an open contest of knowledge and wisdom with Adam. The angels failed in the contest and Adam emerged superior to them in knowledge and wisdom. All of them except Iblis (Satan) obeyed Allah's commandment and bowed down in obedience to Adam.

IBLIS & ADAM

It is said that before the creation of Adam, the earth was inhabited by Jinn, a creation from the elements of fire. They were mutually disruptive and indulged in senseless bloodshed. The angels had referered to their mischief. Iblis was also a Jinn. He was knowledgeable about matters of the earth. By virtue of his devotion and service to Allah, he had secured a high position in the Celectial existence. Iblis had started living with the angels. When Allah ordered all of them to prostrate before Adam, he refused. When asked why he had refused the divine ordinance, he said that he was superior to Adam on several counts. Firstly, his creation came from finer elements. Secondly, he had been in proximity to the Creator in direct servitude. He had vast work experience on the earth where the novice Adam was being sent as a representative. He contended that this was his coveted position and should have been given to him instead to an undeserving novice.

Allah rebuked and down graded Iblis for his disobedience and told him to immediately remove himself from His divine presence and his eternal abode will be reserved in hell inferno. Iblis said that Man was a poor choice for such an important position. He said that he would take every opprtunity to haul all mankind with him to hell. He would like to be granted eternal opportunity to test and tempt this representative and prove that Man may not be such a worthy *khalifa*.

Allah said that only He commands eternity, but He will give him his desired opportunity to the Time known only to Himself. He said that His obedient servents will remain steadfast in all his tough tests and temptations throughout Time, and prove that He created a wise and knowledgeable *khalifa* on earth.

Allah warned Adam about the evil designs of Iblis against him and his progeny throughout Time. But He also assured that those that remain firm in their faith on Truth shall be victorious and will return to Him on the Day of Judgement for a Life of Contentment in close proximity to the Creator.

The Garden of Eden

Allah brought Adam to the Garden of Eden and gave him education towards carrying out the intended functions of *Khalifa on Earth*. Allah created Eve from the substance of Adam as his partner in life and gave them total freedom to enjoy the benevolence of the Provider and Sustainer of Life with prohibition only for a particular tree. The two were not even to go near the tree let alone to taste of its fruit.

Iblis saw his opportunity to tempt Adam and Eve and invoke their curiosity to get closer to the prohibited tree and taste its fruit. No sooner they had done what had been prohibited by the Lord, the Innocense of the Garden of Eden changed to the reality of Life. They heard the voice of their Lord calling. He reminded them of the prohibition He had invoked, which they had clearly transgressed. He reminded them of the open enemosity of Iblis towards them. They were to leave the Garden of Eden and make their abode on

4

the Earth till the end of a period of Time known only to Him. The Almighty said," There you will procreate of your kind in numbers and will colonise the land provided, and eat and drink from that you will procure from the bounties of your Lord. This is where you will spend your lives, and die, and be raised on the Day of Judgement on your conduct on the Earth. Beware of the damaging evil counsel of Iblis who will continue to attempt rift between bretheren, disrupt your lives, cause death and destruction on Earth through those who will listen to him." Both Adam and Eve felt sorry for what they had done, and begged for their forgiveness. Allah reminded them of their role in Life and said that they will return to Him once again to enjoy His bounties in paradise upon their successfully completing the mission on the earth. Thus Adam descended to the earth as a representative of Allah.

The Life and Progeny of Adam

In the beginning, Adam had two sons from Eve named Habeel (Abel) and Qabeel (Cane) followed by Sheeth and others. It is said that Adam lived for almost 930 years.

References: al Qur'an: Surah *Baqrah, Maidah, A'araf, Hajj, Bani Israel, Kahaf, Taha, Saba'a, Yaseen, Jinn and Hajrat.*

PROGENY OF ADAM

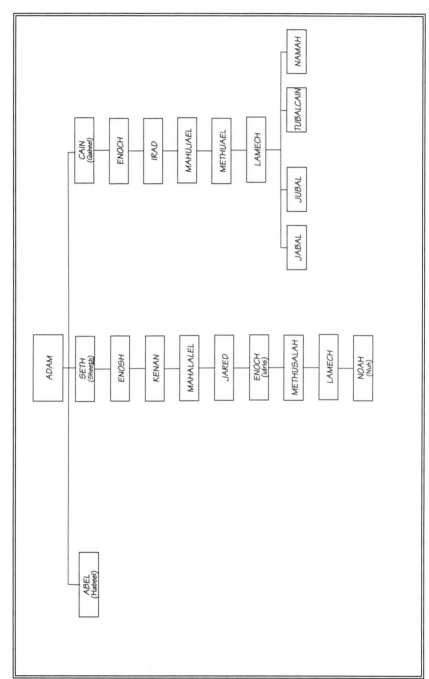

THE STORY OF HABEEL AND QABEEL

It is said that from their first harvest, the two sons of Adam, Habeel and Qabeel, each offered a sacrifice to Allah. The offering of Habeel was accepted for his being " the first among the *muttaqeen* (the God fearing). " A fire descended from the heaven and consumed the offering of Habeel. The offering of Qabeel was spared. He thought that his offering was rejected. This made him jealous of Habeel and he murdered him.

Qabeel felt deep remourse over this act and carried the dead body of his brother over his shoulder, not knowing what to do with it. Then he saw a crow burying a dead crow in the ground. Qabeel followed suit and buried his brother's dead body by digging a hole in the ground.

This was the first criminal act on Earth and it was caused by jealousy. Jealousy is the root cause of many sins, including the murder of fellow human beings. It therefore behoves mankind to avoid this terrible emotion which leads to a lot of sins.

References: al Qur'an: Sura *Maidah*

SHEETH

Adam remained sad after the death of his son Habeel. He had witnessed death for the first time, and was heartbroken at a crime of this magnitude at the hands of his own son against a brother. He was very withdrawn and wept at his predicament. Allah gave him the gift of another son whom he named Sheeth. He succeeded him as a prophet and as a representative of Allah on Earth. He had several children and was the ancestor of the prophets mentioned in the Scriptures.

He is known as Seth in Torah.

IDRIS

Idris was born in the seventh generation from Adam and was the great grand father of Nuh (Noah). He was a great prophet form Allah and was the recipient of numerous revelations from Allah. He is the originator of the art of writing, astrology, astronomy, mathematics, sewing, weights and measures, and many useful instruments and impliments.

It is known that despite his knowledge and piety, the people of his time ignored his teachings and the Lord brought His punishment towards them in the form of a prolonged drought. When they repented, Idris prayed for their forgiveness and the Lord sent down rain to quench the land and swell the rivers for trade and prosperity.

Idris often observed fasting and spent so much of his time in prayers that even the angels in the heavens wondered over his worship. It is said that he was taken away alive by Allah and is kept in occultation by His Will. Idris left a large progeny on Earth from whom Allah chose great leaders and prophets.

He is known as Enoch in Torah.

References: al Qur'an: *Sura Mariam and Anmbiya'*.

NUH

Nuh (Noah) was born to Lamak in the tenth generation of Adam. He was a grand son of Idris. He preached oneness of Allah but the people turned to idolatory. They laughed at Nuh and ridiculed his preaching. They tortured him and his family. Their hearts had hardened and they had shut their ears to his words. Yet he remained patient and continued preaching. When he got tired about the obstinacy and hostility of his people towards him, his family and towards his teachings, he complained to Allah about them. Allah told Nuh that they had transgressed His limits and would meet His punishment which would serve as a lesson for generations to come. He told Nuh that he would send an enormous flood that will engulf and destroy all non-believers and their dwellings along with their false gods.

The Deluge

Allah instructed Nuh to build a large boat and bring on board all believers and a pair of each species of animals before He unleashed His floods. Nuh carried out the instructions of Allah, and started building an enormous ark. Since there were no sea or gulf but only a meager river, people laughed at him for constructing a boat of such large dimensions. Upon completion of his task, Nuh invited people to come on board, but they ridiculed him. The family of the prophet, three of his four sons and a handfull of true believers along with a pair of each species of animals boarded the ark.

9

No sooner Nuh entered the ark, thunderous rain started to pour from the heavens and springs burst from the bottom of the Earth. As the waters rose higher and higher, people climbed up the tallest trees and headed towards high grounds. The waters began to engulf these refuges too. Some people repented and wanted to board the ark, but alas it was too late. The ark had been sealed to protect against the down-pour and the turbulance of the roaring waters. The floods spread far and wide, covering the entire terrain, destroyed all except those who had believed in the prophet, and heeding his warning, had boarded with him.

It is said that the flooding lasted one hundred and fifty days. When the waters receded, the ark came to rest over Mount Ararat. The occupants of the ark came out and thanked the Lord for their miraculous survival. They then spread out to inhabit the Earth again with the blessings of their Lord.

Nuh is known as Noah in Torah. He lived for nine hundred and fifty years and left a large progeny after him. His eldest surviving son Yaffath (Japheth) went north west towards Europe and settled there. His descendents are known as the Japhetic race. His middle son Sam (Shem) remained with his father in the Middle East. His descendents are known as the Semetic race. The youngest son Ham went south west and settled in northern Africa. His descendents are called the Hemetic race.

References: al Qur'an: *Ale Imran, An'am, A'araf, Yunus, Hud, Ibrahim, Bani Israel, Anmbiya',Momenoon, Furqan, Shu'ra', A'nkaboot, Zariyat, Najam, Qamar, Hadeed, Tahreem, Ha'qah and Nuh.*

10

PROGENY OF NUH

NOAH (Nuh)

JAPHETH (Yapheth) — SHEM (Sam) — HAM

EBER
GOMER — ASHKENAZ
MAGOG
JAVAN — TARSHISH

HAM: PUT — CUSH — CANAN
CUSH: NIMROD, SABTAH, RAAMAH, SHEBA, HAVILAH
RAAMAH: SHEBA — DEDAN

SHEM (Sam): ELAM, ASSHUR, ARPAKHSHAD, ARAM
ARPAKHSHAD — SHELAH — EBER — PELEG — REU — SARUG — NAHOR — TERAH — ABRAM (Ibrahim)

EBER: PELEG, JOKTAN
JOKTAN: ALMODAD, HAZERMOVETH, OPHIR, JERAH, DILKAH
SHEBA

ABRAM (Ibrahim): MIDYAN, ISHMAIL (Ismail), ISACC (Ishaq), NAHOR, HARAN
HARAN: LOT (Lut), ISCAH, MILCAH

ADAM
AMIR — AWAIS
THAMUD — A'AD
HAZER — AL KHALUD
OBAID — RUBAH
MASHAY — ABDULLAH
OBAID — HUD
SALEH

HUD

Prophet Hud was born to Shaleh in the fifth generation from Nuh. He was appointed as the messenger from Allah to the people known as Aa'd. These people were a tall and sturdy race. They had abandoned the worship of Allah in favor of idols hewed from stone. Hud preached them the true path for salvation and reminded them of the benevolences that their Creator had bestowed them without their asking. But they refused to pay attention.

Hud warned them of the punishment Allah could unleash over them for their disobedience. They arrogantly rejected his warnings. They thought that no such punishment could ever come over them. They had forgotten the story of the terrible deluge that had come over the people of Nuh for their rejecting of the teachings of their prophet. At first they had to endure a total drought for three years. When Hud tried to ask for their subjugation, they taunted him: "Go ahead and do whatever you could, because we consider you only a fool."

When Allah saw those people paid no heed to His signs, a terrible storm overtook them for an overwhelming duration of eight days. There was an utter darkness, and debris flew in all directions. The whole nation of these arrogant people perished, and Hud and only a small group of believers were saved by the Grace and benevolence of Allah.

11

He is known as A'eeber or A'aber in Torah.

References: al Qur'an: Sura: *A'araf, Hud, Ibrahim, Furqan, Shu'ra', A'nkaboot, Ha-Meem Sajdah, Ahqaf, Zariyat, Najan, Qamar, Alhaqah and Fajar.*

SALEH

Saleh was born in the ninth generation from Nuh. He was appointed prophet for the Thamud people who inhabited the moutanous territory between Hejaz and Palestine. They built their homes by hewing the rocky faces of cliffs. They lived long lives and worshiped gods made from stone.

They refused to listen to the wisdom of Saleh and challenged him to show them any sign to prove that an invisible God existed. They demanded a miracle at their annual festival. They told Saleh: "You pray to your God and we will pray to ours. Let us see whose prayer is accepted, yours or ours. That will decide the matter between us."

They came in drones from around the land and gathered around their decorated stone gods and brought offerings for fulfilments of their prayers. Clearly the stone gods were unable to respond to their prayers. They then turned to Saleh and one of them asked him to pray to his God and to bring out a pregnant camel from the large boulder that was lying on the ground, and if this she-camel had an off-spring born in front of their eyes, they would accept Saleh's God as theirs as well.

Saleh prayed to The Almighty Allah and sure enough a pregnant she-camel rose out of the large boulder and gave birth to a calf as they watched. They were clearly struck with wonder on this miracle.

13

In accordance with Allah's Command, Saleh told the people that they must share their drink with the camel. It was agreed that the people would use the water from the village well on all days of the week except one day which was reserved for the camel and her baby. But they were a disobedient people. They refused the animals to drink or graze freely in the territory as agreed, and forced Saleh to assume their full responsibility. Saleh told them that the camel and her baby were there because they had asked for the miracle, and they must take care of the animals. They threatened to kill the two animals. He then reminded them of the benevolence of Allah that only He could bestow over His creation without asking for it, namely water, rain, fertility of the land where crops grow, the stone cliffs where they built their homes, and the clean air that they breathed. They must refrain from their threatened acts otherwise they would bring down a disaster over themselves.

One day the people carried out their threat and slew both the mother and her baby camel. This invited Allah's immediate wrath.

Allah instructed Saleh to leave the territory along with his family and a small group of true believers before His wrath would strike that insolent people. No sooner the pious group of believers had crossed over the last of the cliffs, than a tremendous earth quake shook the land with a blinding lightning and an ear shattering thunder. The entire people in that territory perished along with their false gods.

References: al Qur'an: *Sura A'raf, Hud, Ibrahim, Hajar, Furqan, Shu'ra', Nahl, A'nkaboot, Ha-Meem Sajdah, Zariyat, Qamar, al-Ha'qah, Fajar, Shams.*

IBRAHIM

The Birth of Ibrahim

Ibrahim was born in the fifth generation from Hud, and during the reign of a tyrant known as Namrood (Nimrod). Namrood, a powerful king, made his subjects bow to him as a god. One night he dreamt that a star rose from the horizon and its brilliance eclipsed the moon and the sun. He woke up wondering about the interpretation of his dream. He summoned the astrologers and fortune tellers to come up with the most acceptable explanation of his dream. They conferred with one another and told him: 'A person will be born in your kingdom who will wreck your power and destroy your influence.' He asked if that person had actually been born or would be born in the near future. They told him that he was not yet born. Upon hearing that, Namrood ordered a ban on all marriages, separating men from women and ordered the killing of all new borns.

Allah is All Powerful and All Knowing. His intentions come to be whenever He deems them to be. The mother of Ibrahim successfully concealed her pregnancy. She went out of the city limits and gave birth to her child in a cave. She stayed in that cave with her child until the senseless slaughter of the new borns had come to an end and the king's own fear of his destruction had abated. By this time Ibrahim had grown up to be a tall and handsome lad. They returned to their ancestral home in the city of Ur.

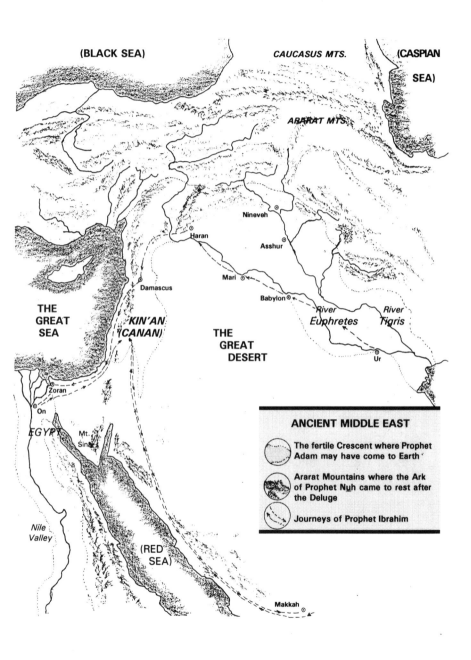

(BLACK SEA)

CAUCASUS MTS.

(CASPIAN SEA)

ARARAT MTS.

Nineveh

Haran

Asshur

Mari

Damascus

Babylon

THE GREAT SEA

KIN'AN (CANAN)

River Euphretes

River Tigris

THE GREAT DESERT

Ur

Zoran

On

EGYPT

Mt. Sinai

Nile Valley

(RED SEA)

Makkah

ANCIENT MIDDLE EAST

The fertile Crescent where Prophet Adam may have come to Earth

Ararat Mountains where the Ark of Prophet Nuh came to rest after the Deluge

Journeys of Prophet Ibrahim

His Intelligence, Cognition, and Rejection of Idolatory:

In those days people believed in the celestial bodies as their deities. One night, Ibrahim also selected the brightest of all the stars for his observation. By the morning its light faded and it disappeared. He thought that the most brilliant of the stars could not be the creator as it faded away in the brightness of another celetial body. Similarly he noted that the moon changed phases, and was but a shadow in front of the brightness of the sun. He concluded that the moon could not be the creator either. He pondered if the sun were the ultimate god, as he had also noted people bowing in subjugation to the sun. But the sun was out only for the duration of the day, and gave way to the stars and the moon at night. He reflected upon this phenomenon and concluded that the one who put these celestial bodies in their respective places has the supreme power over them and must be the God Almighty, even though He were not visible or physically tangible. He was pleased with this conclusion and enthusiastically began to tell people how wrong they all had been to ignore the obvious power behind their daily lives, the Supreme power of Allah. He invited them to give up their false gods and return to the truth.

Some laughed at his idea, some ignored him as he was only a youth "with little knowledge of life," while others were offended and admonished him for his lack of respect for their gods.

They invited him to come to the annual festival and see for himself how they had decorated their gods along with fabulous offerings brought over from far and wide. Ibrahim excused himself and did not go to the festival. As the towns people had all gone to the fair grounds to indulge in their

16

festivities, Ibrahim went to their temple, broke all their idols and left his axe hanging on the shoulder of the biggest of them all in the center of the temple.

Next day when people went to the temple and saw what had happened to their gods, they knew that Ibrahim had done it, since he had made no secret of his dislike of those idols. The village chief asked Ibrahim if he knew who had broken their idols. Ibrahim, pointing towards the big idol said, "Why don't you ask him?" The cheif said, "How could a stone idol do such a deed?" There upon Ibrahim said, "If the stone idol was incapable of doing it, or protect itself and the other idols, how could it be a god, the provider and the protector?" They obviously had no answer to the logic of Ibrahim. However, they were not prepared to follow his path. They wanted him punished for being disrespectful to their gods. They sent a deputation to Namrood, their god-king for a judgement against Ibrahim.

Ibrahim was summoned to the court of Namrood to answer his charges and face the punishment.

When all the people had gathered in the court, Namrood arrived. All subjects bowed down to the ground for their total submission except for Ibrahim who remained upright and did not bow to the king-god. When asked why he refused to bow to him, Ibrahim replied that he submitted only to his God, The Creator, The Sustainer. This was an open insult to the king who commanded an absolute power over his subjects and claimed himself to be a god. By his act, Ibrahim had provoked the king's wrath. However, surprised at the courage of Ibrahim, the king decided to question him.

Debate in the Court of Namrood on the existance of Allah

The king asked Ibrahim to explain to the entire audience who his god was. Ibrahim said that his God was one who gave life and who took it away. The king said that he did that every day!

Ibrahim said that his God brought forth the sun from the east. He asked the king that if he had the power, could he cause the sun to rise from the west! Clearly the king was unable to carry out such a feat.

The king then turned around and asked Ibrahim why he had broken all the idols in the temple. He gave the same reply to the king as he had given to the chief of the village before. The king said to Ibrahim that he knew that the idols did not talk and yet he kept on referring to the biggest of them to answer the question that actually pertained to him. Ibrahim said that since the king and all his subjects knew that idols did not talk why then they worshiped them as gods.

As there were no answers to the logic of Ibrahim the king ordered his courtiers to dig a large pit, light a wood fire and throw Ibrahim in it alive, to make an example so that nobody would again disobey or ridicule their god-king.

The Miraculous escape of Ibrahim from the fire

The pit was dug and a large fire was lit in it. When it was roaring with flames and the heat could be felt from a distance, Ibrahim was thrown in it. Ibrahim prayed to the true God, Allah, for His mercy in that hour of trial. By the Grace of Allah neither the fire nor the heat touched Ibrahim. He walked around as if in a garden and left the pit totally unharmed. This indeed was a miracle that convinced some of the onlookers who bowed to the true God and accepted the true religion of Allah and gave up idolatory.

Ibrahim left his ancestoral city of Ur and migrated north to Haran where he stayed for a short period of time. Then he moved west to Kin'an (Canan in Torah), along with his wife Sarah and nephew Lut (Lot in Torah). After a while, Lut was appointed messenger by Allah to the people of Sidom and Gomorrah who lived north of Kin'an.

The Progeny of Ibrahim

Before finally settling in Kin'an, Ibrahim visited Egypt where the king gave him a maiden (according to some, his daughter) in marriage. Her name was Hajirah (Hager in Torah). Allah gave Ismail as the first born child to Ibrahim through his second wife Hajirah at a old age of eighty six years. Sarah was infertile and became jealous of Hajirah. Under instructions from Allah, Ibrahim took his son Ismail and his wife Hajirah from Kin'an and brought them down south in the land of Arabia where they were left to live for rest of their lives. Ismail grew up to be a handsome and tall young man who had many children and is popularly known as the patriarch of the Arabs.

Back in Kin'an, after a few years, Sarah who had grown old, and given up hope of ever bearing a child of her own, also conceived and bore a son to Ibrahim named Ishaq. It is worth noting here that Ibrahim had then turned ninety nine years of age. Ishaq was a great prophet of Allah in the land of Kin'an. He remained settled in Kin'an and had several prominent prophets amongst his progeny.

After the death of his wife Sarah, Ibrahim took another wife named Qutura from whom had many sons and daughters. These children of Ibrahim settled and populated the lands of Madain, Midyan and Saba.

The Trial of Ibrahim by Allah

One night Ibrahim saw in his dream that he had sacrificed his son Ismail to please Allah. He wondered over this dream and pondered over its meaning. He saw the same dream on three consecutive nights. He called his son Ismail and told him about his dreams. The son asked his father to do exactly what he had seen in his dreams, if that was the wish of the Creator Almighty, and that he would find him patient. Ibrahim tied his son just as he would tie a sacrificial lamb, and placed the knife on the throat of his son to carry out the sacrifice. The Sustainer of life and of all mankind sent the archangel Jibril (Gabrial) with salutations from Allah and told the father and the son that their belief in Allah and their resolve to give their most valued possession in life in His way had pleased Him greatly. Allah had sent a lamb to be sacrificed in place of Ismail. Ibrahim thanked the Lord for the acceptance of his service and returned home with humility and gratitude towards Allah. This act of Ibrahim has been perpetuated by Allah for ever, and is celebrated by Muslims all over the world every year when they sacrifice a lamb. This event is known as Eid-al-Adha.

The Construction of Ka'ba and Hajj

Ibrahim and his son Ismail built the Ka'ba and inserted the Black Stone in one of the corners of the building in accordance with the Will of Allah. The ritual of Hajj was initiated at that time and has continued to this day.

Solution to the question of Death and Resurrection

Once Ibrahim asked Allah how would He bring them to life again when the living had died and perished. Allah asked Ibrahim if he had doubts over that question. He said he had no doubt about the absolute powers of his Lord but he wanted to satisfy his curiosity over the mechanism of resurrection.

Allah instructed Ibrahim: 'gather four birds, let them become familiar with you, then sacrifice them, mix their meat and scatter it on four hills across from one another. Then call the birds by their names, and they will come to you.' Ibrahim did as instructed, and verily the same happened as predicted by the Supreme One, Allah. Thus Ibrahim solved the riddle of resurrection of the dead on the Day of Judgement. Allah will call His creation as He Wills, and they will all rise from their graves.

The Ritual of Circumcision

When Ibrahim turned ninety nine years of age, Allah ordained that he himself, his male progeny, and all believers be circumcised. The divine order was obeyed. It might be noted here that Ishaq was born to Ibrahim at that old age and after the ritual of circumcision. This ritual is practiced by the Muslims and the Jews, the followers of Ibrahim, and all those who recognize the hygienic advantages of circumcision.

The Death of Ibrahim

This great prophet and a friend of Allah, also known as the patriarch of all subsequent prophets, died at the age of one hundred and seventy five years.

Major Lessons from the Life of Ibrahim

1.   Do not remain ignorant about religion, nor be stubborn about the old ways of our forefathers. Seek the truth. Accept it when discovered.

2.   Do not associate any thing or any one with The Creator. Nothing can share with Him the glory of His Oneness.

3.   Submit to Allah in total submission to enjoy His bounty and benevolence.

4.   When it is difficult to practice your faith in safety and in peace, move to another place, for His territory is vast and His bounty limitless.

5.   Whenever occasions arise requiring sacrifice to preserve or protect Faith, do not hesitate, for all we have, came from Him. We are independent owners of nothing in this world.

References: al Qur'an: *Sura Baqra, ale Imran, Nisa', An'am, Taubah, Hud, Yusuf, Ibrahim, Hajar, Nahl, Mariyam, Anmbiya'a, Hajj, Shu'ra'a, A'nkaboot, Sa'fat, Jinn, Zakhraf, Hadeed, Mumtahna, Zariyat, Najam, Taha.*

LUT

Lut was a nephew of Ibrahim, born to his brother name Haran in the city of Ur. Haran had died when Ibrahim quit Ur, and Lut accompanied his uncle Ibrahim in his travels. When Ibrahim finally settled in Kin'an, Allah appointed Lut as His messenger to the people inhabiting the northern vally of River Jordan, in the region of Motaffakah. There were two prosperous cities in this region known as Sodom and Gomorrah.

The people living in this region were morally corrupt. They openly practiced homosexuality. They defied the teachings of Lut and ridiculed and tortured him. In fact the degree of defiance was so high that Lut and his family lived in constant threat of persecution.

The Destruction of Sodom and Gomorrah

It was the year when Allah sent instructions to Ibrahim for ritual circumcision. He received Angels who informed him of the doom that was in stock for the people of Sidom and Gomorrah. Ibrahim asked for the safety of his nephew Lut and his family. After assurances from Allah about the safety of his nephew and his family, the angels left for the territory of the ill fated people.

The angels arrived at the door of Lut in the form of handsome lads. The towns people rushed to grab them for their pleasure. Lut pleaded for their release but failed due to their superior numbers and determination. The angels delivered the instructions from Allah to Lut and told him to quit the region immediately and none of them should look back.

No sooner the family of Lut had climbed the hills beyond the territory of Sodom and Gomorrah, than a terrible earth quake struck the region. A fire of sulphur and huge boulders flung from above and from the bowels of the earth, fully destroying the people and the two cities. The wife of Lut sympathized with the sinful people and disobeyed the instructions of Allah. She turned back to look at the raging destruction down in the valley and was converted to a pillar of rock. Lut hurried out of the region with rest of his family to the sanctuary promised by Allah.

References: al Qur'an: *Sura An'am, A'raf, Hud, Hajar, Anmbiya', Shu'ra', Nahl, A'nkaboot, Sa'faat, Zariyat, Najan, Qamar, Tahreem.*

ISMAIL

Ismail was the elder son of Ibrahim born to Hajirah. Sarah, the first wife of Prophet Ibrahim had no child of her own. She became jealous of Hajirah. But Allah had his own designs for Sarah. Allah instructed Ibrahim to take his wife Hajirah and his son Ismail to Hejaz, deep south in the desert of Arabia where the city of Makkah stands today. It was a desolate place at that time.

The Miracle of Zam Zam

The place where Allah had instructed Ibrahim to leave his wife and child was without any vegetation or habitation. Ismail was thirsty and the mother had run out of water. She ran several times between two hills trying to look out for help, water or vegetation. She was unsuccessful in her quest. However as the child cried kicking the ground with his heels, a spring of fresh water gushed out. This spring runs with unlimited fresh water to this day, and is treated as holy water by pilgrims to Makkah. The act of Hajirah became so significant in her effort to save the life of her child who would be a prophet, that Allah deemed this an essential part of the Hajj ritual for all times to come.

The Founding of the City of Makkah

A wandering tribe of the land known as Banu Jarham arrived in the desolate territory to find Ismail and his mother encamped with the fresh water spring which never existed there before. They were fascinated when they heard the story

25

of the spring. They knew that there had been no such spring at that site before. They paid reverence to the holy family and erected their tents by the spring. This temporary sojourn became a permanent settlement, and later came to be known as Makkah.

The Trial of Ibrahim by Allah

Ismail was only nine when his father Ibrahim saw in a dream, that he sacrificed his only son to please Allah. On seeing the same dream on three consecutive nights, he told Ismail about it. Ismail replied that it must be a test from Allah to test their wills, and he was willing to be sacrificed in the way of Allah. Ibrahim took his son Ismail to Mina, laid him on the ground, and tied his arms and legs with a cord. As he placed his knife on the throat of his son, the Archangel Jibril (Gabrial) appeared and announced that the test of their ultimate submission to Allah was complete. Just then, by the Grace of Allah, a healthy lamb appeared there to be sacrificed in place of Ismail. Ibrahim was given the happy tiding that Allah was pleased with them, and their position would be elevated. Ibrahim was also given the happy news of another son, Ishaq.

This act of the great prophet Ibrahim and his son Ismail became an essential part of Hajj for all times, and is celebrated a day before the annual Eid al-Adha'.

The Building of Ka'ba

Ibrahim and his son Ismail, following divine instructions, built the Ka'ba in Makkah as a House of worship for Allah. On completion of the Holy structure, both of them prayed to Allah for acceptance of their service. They called upon the people to come for pilgrimage (Hajj). Since then, the tradition of the two prophets has continued to be performed through the centuries. The black stone *(Hajre Aswad)* was placed in one corner of the building by the Prophet Ibrahim. According to some traditions, this stone had descended from the heaven!

For the muslim pilgrim, one of the center points of the rituals of Hajj is to go round the Ka'ba seven times and to kiss Hajre Aswad. This is done in remembrance to the act of devotion by the patriarch of our prophets. It is one of the essential obligations of the faithful to go to Makkah and perform the ritual Hajj at least once during his life time.

Ismail had many sons and daughters who migrated to several parts of the Arabian peninsula and they imparted the teachings of Ibrahim wherever they settled. However Makkah remained the central place of congregation throughout the ages, and Ka'ba continued to be the most revered house of worship.

Ismail is also known as *Abul Arab*, the patriarch of the Arabs.

The last of the messengers of Allah, the Prophet of Islam, Muhammad, was born in the clan of Quraish who descended from Ismail and were amongst the most powerful people of Arabia.

References: al Qur'an: *Sura Baqara, An'am, Maryam, An'mbiya', Sa'ffat, Jinn.*

27

ISHAQ

Ishaq was born to Sarah the first wife of Ibrahim nine years after the birth of Ismail to Hajirah. In fact the news of the birth of the second son was given to Ibrahim after passing the trial of the sacrifice of his son Ismail in Mina'. Ishaq lived in Kin'an and was appointed prophet towards his people by Allah. He had two sons, who were twins. They were named Issau and Ya'qub (Jacob). Banu Israil are named after Ya'qub who was also known as Israil.

References: al Qur'an: Sura Baqarah, An'am, Yusuf, Anmbiya', Sa'ffat, Jinn.

YA'QUB

Ya'qub was one of the twin sons of Ishaq. He was appointed prophet towards his people after the death of his father. His popular name was Israil, and his progeny is called Banu Israil (the children of Israil).

He had twelve sons and one daughter. The twelve tribes of the children of Israil are named after his twelve sons. Yusuf was one of his sons. He was extremely handsome and was dearly loved by his father. His brothers were jealous of him and they always looked for an excuse to get him away from their father. Finally they took him away at the pretext of hunting and threw him in a well. Ya'qub cried so much at the separation of his beloved son that he lost his eye sight.

As will be seen in the narrative on the life of Yusuf, Allah rescued Yusuf from the well and made him the king of Egypt. There was famine in the land of Kin'an, and his brothers came to get grain from the king. Yusuf recognized them, for they were the same fellows who had thrown him in the well. He forgave them and had them move, along with his father, to Egypt.

The children of Israil remained in Egypt for about four hundred and thirty years until Musa ultimately rescued them from the ill treatment rendered by King Rameses III.

References: al Qur'an: *Sura Baqara, An'am, Ale Imran, Yusuf, Anmbiya', Jinn, Momen.*

29

YUSUF

Yusuf was one of the twelve sons of Ya'qub. His mother's name was Raheel. He had a younger sister and a brother named Benyamin (Benjamin) from the same mother. Yusuf was exceptionally handsome and was very dear to his parents.

The dream of Yusuf and its interpretation by his father

One day Yusuf told his father about a dream he had seen the previous night. He saw that the sun, the moon and eleven stars bowed down before him. His father was the prophet of the time and knew the meaning of the dream. He told him that he would be a prophet of Allah and will be a powerful king over all, including his parents and his brothers.

Ill treatment of Yusuf by his brothers

Interpretation of the dream by Ya'qoub did not sit well with his sons who were already distraught due to their father's special affections for Yusuf. They decided to get rid of their brother Yusuf. They threw him in a well and brought his shirt, smothered in sheep's blood. They put up a false scene upon entering their home, wailing and crying. They told their parents that a wolf had devouvered their young brother, and that they were unable to save him from the terrible fate.

Ya'qub was so grieved at the story and was so saddened by the apparent loss of his son that he wept profusely all day and all night. It is said that he lost his eye sight due to excessive crying.

Yusuf retrieved from the well and sold as a slave

Having thrown their younger brother in the well, the older brothers stayed around to see what may happen. A caravan headed for Egypt stopped at the well, for water and rest. Seeing a handsome youth in the well they pulled him out and wondered at his beauty and youth. The brothers showed up in front of the leader of the caravan and said that the youth was their slave who had escaped from them and had hidden himself in the well. The leader of the caravan saw the potential of higher sale value for Yusuf in the slave market of Egypt and he paid a lowly price to his brothers for legitimising his ownership.

Upon arriving in Egypt, the caravan leader placed Yusuf on the market. His price increased every day. The ruler of Egypt heard about the sale of an exceptionally handsome youth in his city and he came down to see him. He was stunned at the beauty of the lad and paid the highest price at the bidding. He took him to his palace to serve his beautiful wife, Zulaikhah who had no child.

Yusuf in servitude of the Pharaoh of Egypt

Yusuf served the king and his wife with such honesty and efficiency that he was made incharge of the ruler's house-hold. It so happened that Zulaikhah developed infatuation for Yusuf and started to love him with increasing passion.

31

The story of Zulaikhah's love for Yusuf

Zulaikhah fell madly in love with Yusuf, but he took every opportunity to avoid her advances. At one occasion she was successful in trapping him into her chamber so that she could be alone with him. No sooner he realized the wicked designs of the queen than he made for the door of the chamber. She lunged after him and was able to grab his shirt from behind. In the short scuffle that followed, Yusuf's shirt was torn from behind. Just as he escaped through the chamber door, he bumped into the king himself. Realizing the acuteness of her situation, the queen yelled out for help. The ruler was greatly angered by the rather strange circumstances and looked at Yusuf demanding an explanation. Yusuf said that he was innocent, and that Zulaikhah was the guilty one. One of Zulaikhah's own relatives from the house-hold came forward to clear the matter. He said that if Yusuf's shirt was torn from front, then he was the aggressor and culpable for his actions, but if it was torn from behind, then Zulaikhah was guilty. As Yusuf's shirt was torn from behind, the ruler found his wife to be culpable for the embarrassing event.

He told Yusuf to forget the event, and told his wife to refrain from seeing Yusuf when alone. However, the story of the scandel got out of the palace, and spread far and wide. Women of other nobles maliciously gossiped about this happening.

Zulaikhah arranged a party and invited the women of nobility to her palace. As they were busy cutting and eating fruits, she summoned Yusuf into her audience. As he arrived in their presence, the women got totally stunned by his beauty, and many cut their fingers instead of the fruits in their hands. They were now convinced over what they had heard about Yusuf and his beauty.

Yusuf prayed to Allah to save him from the wickedness of the queen and other women of Egypt.

The imprisonment of Yusuf

When the king learnt about the scandalous involvement of the wives of other nobles in his kingdom over Yusuf, he considered it best to take Yusuf away from his palace, and threw him into the prison. However the supervisor of the prisons noted the purity of character and conduct of Yusuf and started to treat him with respect. He made him his deputy in managing the affairs of the prison.

Interpretation of dreams by Yusuf

It so happened that two other young men were thrown in the same prison. Each one of them saw a dream. One saw that he was extracting juice from ripe grapes and the other saw that he was carrying a basket of bread over his head, and birds ate freely from it. They asked Yusuf if he could interpret their dreams. He gave them sermon on virtuous conduct and belief on the oneness of Allah. He then gave them the interpretation of their dreams. He told the one who saw himself extracting juice from grapes, that he would be pardoned for the allegations and would be set free, and that he would return to his old employment of serving drinks to his master. He told the other intern that he would be crucified for his deeds, and birds of prey would feed on his corp after his death. Yusuf then asked the first prisoner to make a plea for his release as soon as he got out of the prison. But the man forgot his promise.

33

Now the king saw a dream over successive nights that got him concerned. His courtiers and astrologers failed to satisfy him with any plausable interpretation. At that time, one of the prisoners who had survived, remembered Yusuf. He told the ruler that he could find the interpretation of his dreams if he was allowed to visit Yusuf in the prison. He was permitted to do so.

He greeted Yusuf and narrated the dream to him. The ruler, in his dream, had seen seven fat cows emerging from the river, followed by seven weak ones. The weak cows devoured the fat ones. He then saw seven green and healthy ears of wheat followed by seven dry ones. The dry ones ate up the green ones.

Yusuf said that both the dreams had the same interpretation. The seven fat cows and the seven healthy ears consist of seven years during which the country would see high productivity. That would be followed by seven years of femine. Unless the years of high productivity were managed wisely, the years of femine would totally destroy the kingdom. He told the ruler that it would be prudent to save for the years of femine, for the femine would be wide spread.

The ruler carefully listened to the interpretation of his dreams by Yusuf, and he knew that it must be true. He called Yusuf back to his court and restored his position with full respect. Zulaikhah , by now had admitted her mistake.

Yusuf rises to the highest status in Egypt

The ruler made Yusuf the chief administrator of the country's produce. He gave Yusuf his ring that testified his total authority on his behalf. Yusuf was only thirty years of age at that time. He went straight to work and began the implementation of methods to enhance the produce. He built large graineries for storage. He conserved resources over expenditure, in preparation for the bad times he had predicted.

Brothers of Yusuf in Egypt

As foretold, femine srtuck the land of Egypt as well as the lands arround Egypt. The news of the graineries of Egypt had already spread far and wide. People flocked to Egypt for jobs and food. Thus Egypt flourished with cheap labor even during the days of wide spread femine. This was a clear sign of the intelligence and foresight of Yusuf.

Like other lands, femine visited the land of Kin'an as well. Ya'qub sent his sons to Egypt to procure grain. When they came in the presence of Yusuf in their wretched attire, they could not recognise their own brother who was wearing his royal attire and had grown into handsome manhood. But Yusuf recognised them. He gave them love, affection, shelter and food, but did not reveal his identity to them. He asked them about their family and they told him about his father who had lost his eye sight from crying over the loss of his beloved son. When they were leaving with grain. Yusuf insisted that they had to leave one of them as security. They must also bring their youngest brother when they return or else they would not be given additional grain. They had no choice and one of them had to stay in Egypt.

Yusuf's brothers returned to Egypt with their youngest brother Benyamin, who was his sibling from the same mother. They brought the price of the previous cargo, and gifts from their old and ailing father. The reminiscence of his childhood and separation from his beloved parents made Yusuf cry. He revealed his identity to his brothers and sent them back laden with gifts and grain. He invited them to come and live in Egypt, as the femine was to last for a few years.

They returned to Egypt with their parents as well as other members of their clan. They bowed to him as subjects do before the king. This indeed was the true interpretation of the dream that Yusuf had had as a child. Although his brothers had reacted to that dream with such cruelty, yet Yusuf paid them back with sympathy, love and forgiveness.

The death of Ya'qub

Ya'qub lived for seventeen years in Egypt before his death. He called his sons at his death bed and advised them on matters of their mutual benefit and wished that upon his death that his body should be carried back to Kin'an for burial near his forefathers. His wishes were carried out with royal ceremonials.

The death of Yusuf

Yusuf lived for one hundred and ten years. He was buried in Egypt according to the rituals of the land, and when Musa finally took the children of Israil out of Egypt, he took the coffin of Yusuf to Kin'an, to be buried alongside his ancestors

References: al Qur'an: *Sura Yusuf, Mo'min.*

SHO'AYB

Sho'ayb was a direct descendant of Ibrahim from his later wife named Quturah. He was appointed prophet by Allah to the people of Midyan and Aykah, who lived on the east of Mount Sinai. He was the father-in-law of Musa, who had taken refuge with him after the Pharaoh of Egypt had banished him into the Sinai desert.

The people of Midyan and Aykah cheated on weights and measures. They waylaid caravans and were corrupt morally. They jeered at the teachings of Sho'ayb and challenged him to show them what he meant by the punishment of Allah, if indeed there was such a God. Their insolence reached such heights that Allah sent His wrath upon them which they had demanded. The people of Midyan were destroyed by roaring thunder and violent earth quakes. The people of Aykah were covered with darkness that emitted fire, destroying most living beings. None except for a handful of true believers survived these calamities.

References: al Qur'an: *Sura A'araf, Hud, Hajar, Shu'ra', and A'nkaboot.*

MUSA

The Birth and Early Life of Musa

The children of Israil came to Egypt during the days of Yusuf and flourished with wealth and large progenies. Their growth in wealth and power became a threat to the rulers of Egypt. The adviser of the pharaohs devised several ways to reduce this threat. This brought great hardship to the children of Israil. Around the time of the birth of Musa there were rumors that a great messiah will be born that year amongst these people and that he will challenge the might of the Pharaoh and liberate the children of Israil. The Pharaoh ordered all male babies born to these people to be killed so that the messiah may never challenge his power. This was extremely painful for the parents of many ill-fated infants that were slain as a result of this cruel decree.

Allah has His Divine Wisdom and no body can avert what He has planned or designed.

Musa was born in the house of Imran, in the clan of Lavi (one of the twelve clans of Banu Israil). Fearful of the destiny of her child at the hands of the rulers of the time, his mother laid him in a basket and set on the waters of the mighty Nile. The basket drifted towards the gardens surrounding the palace of the Phraoh. The maids in attendance to queen retrieved the basket and saw a beautiful baby in it. The queen who had no child of her own developed immediate love for the baby. She adopted him as her son. He was named Musa, which, in the old Egyptian language meant "pulled out of water."

Allah has His own ways of protecting and providing for His chosen servants.

The hungry baby needed to be fed but he did not accept any of the fostered mothers brought in. The sister of Musa had followed the basket to the palace. She offered to bring one of the new mothers whose baby had recently been slain. She did not reveal her or her mother's association with the baby. The queen agreed, as she had no other choice. When the mother of Musa was presented in the palace as one who had been deprived of her baby, Musa responded immediately to the nursing. The queen hired her to nurse the baby in the palace and at her own home as needed. The infant prophet, a servant of Allah was thus returned to his own mother and household for care and nurture.

Musa as a teenager in the palace of Pharaoh

The Pharaoh saw the intellectual brilliance in this youth and appointed his top astrologers, magicians, scribes and priests to educate Musa in all aspects of the royal faculties. He must have intended to appoint Musa as his special advisor, or high priest, or even his successor. However, this could also be the Will of Allah to have Musa gain all the secrets of the Pharaoh that made him so powerful.

Musa in the service of Sho'ayb

Musa was naturally inclined to help his people. One

day, while trying to free an Israilite in a scuffle with an Egyptian, Musa killed the Egyptian with one blow. This incidence reached the elite circle of the ruling class who branded Musa as a friend of the wretched Israilites whom the Egyptians hated from the core of their hearts. They passed a unanimous resolution to have a public trial of Musa to get him killed for his deed against an Egyptian. A noble person in the clan of the Pharaoh (called *Mo'mine Ale-Fir'on* in Qur'an) informed Musa of the plot and he helped him escape into the desert.

The desert journey was arduous. Musa reached the city of Midyan. He came to rest at a well where several shephards were busy watering their herds. He saw that there were two young and beautiful women waiting for their turn to serve their herd. The men took their turns assertively while the ladies waited patiently. Musa could not remain passive at the sight. He offered to help the young women by pulling the water from the well. They told him that their father was old and since he was unable to do this work, they had no choice but to come out to serve their herd. Sometimes it could be quite late in the evening when they returned to their home.

Musa helped them water their herd expeditiously, and they returned home early. Their father enquired on their unusual early return. They told him of the incidence at the well. Sho'ayb recognized the deed to be that of a man of Allah and sent one of his daughters to bring him home. Musa had nowhere else to go, so he accompanied the lady to her home. Sho'ayb asked Musa the details of his travel. The story of Musa fascinated all in the audience. Sho'ayb offered Musa to stay with him, and married one of his daughters to him. He lived in the clan for about ten years and led an extemely simple life in contrast to the comforts of the royal Egyptian palace. He tended the sheep and goats of the family and spent time in the solitude of the desert. Here he contemplated and reflected on his past and present experiences. He had discusssions with his father-in-law, Sho'ayb which enriched him spiritually. He reflected over the plight of his people in Egypt and made a firm resolve to free them from the servitude of the Egyptians.

The Prophethood of Musa and his return to Egypt

After living ten years in Midyan, Musa left for Egypt, accompanied by his family. On their way, one night, they pitched their tents near Mount Sinai. It was cold and they needed fire for warmth. He saw what looked like a fire higher up on the mountain. Musa told the family to stay in the tents while he would go up the mountain to bring the fire for their comfort.

When he arrived at the site, instead of fire, he noticed a brilliant light emanating from a bush. Musa approached the bush cautiously when he heard a voice calling him to take off his shoes as he was in the presence of his Creator, and that he was standing on the santified terraine. It was here that Allah bestowed upon Musa the gifts of miracles to be used while confronting the mighty Pharaoh. He was given a brilliant light in his hand (*Yade-baiza*), and a staff with miraculous powers. Allah told him that He would give him other great signs to help accomplish His mission. Musa was then instructed to proceed to Egypt immediately.

Musa said that he was afraid of getting arrested on a previous murder charge, and also because he could not speak fluently due to his stuttering. He prayed to Allah to grant him fluency of speech, and have his brother Harun help him and be a deputy to him in all his tasks ahead. Allah granted Musa his requests and told him that he could take his brother along with him, and told him to be gentle in his language and be patient in all his dealings.

Musa was overwhelmed at the experience. The brilliant light emanating from the bush disappeared. For his own satisfaction, Musa varified the miracles of *Yade-baiza* and conversion of his staff into a serpent. He knew that it was not a dream, and he indeed was in the presence of The Divine One.

Musa came down from the mountain, narrated his experience to his wife, who acnowledged him to be the prophet of Allah and gave him the reassurance and comfort he needed. They made their way to Egypt, and to the house of Imran, his father. He took Harun aside and told him of his appointment as a prophet and his vicergeant. Harun was pleased and assured to help his brother in the task that lay ahead.

The confrontation with the Pharaoh

Musa and Harun arrived in the court of the Pharaoh and told him that his claim of godhood was false, for there is but one God who created the king and the subject. He controls all that is in this world and beyond. The only reason for his return to Egypt was to obtain the release of his people from their bondage in Egypt.

The Pharaoh was not pleased with the dialogue, and said that Musa was a fugitive of their law and was to be hanged for the crime of killing an Egyptian. Musa said that the final justice was in the hands of Allah and that the Pharaoh himself was commiting the worst crime in defying his own Creator by forcing his false godhood over his subjects. Musa produced the miracle of *Yadebaiza*, and showed how, with the Will of Allah, his hand could produce blinding brilliance. The Pharaoh laughed and said that was nothing but an act of magic. To impress Musa, his magicians threw strings on the floor which turned into snakes. Musa threw his staff to the floor. It became a serpent and devoured all the wriggling snakes.

Whereas the magic of the Pharaoh was beaten, he declined to acknowledge the superiority of Allah over him. As he defiantly refused to allow Bani Israil to leave Egypt, Musa had to unleash the punishment of Allah over him and his people. These punishments came in the form of unseasonal floods that demolished their dwellings, swarms of locust that destroyed the crop, pestilence of lice that made life miserable, toads that croaked and sprang everywhere, and the turning of all driking water into blood. Each time the Pharaoh was subjected to humiliation, his defiance became pervasive. Finally, when the first born sons of all Egyptians started to die from no apparent cause, including the beloved son of the Pharaoh, he finally gave up his defiance and most reluctantly agreed Bani Israil to leave Egypt.

The Exodus of Bani Israil from Egypt

Musa issued specific instructions for his people to collect all their belongings and leave their homes before sun rise, to gather outside the city periphery. The remains of Yusuf had already been collected in a coffin box, which was

43

hauled out of the city, with caution and respect. As the people had little time to cook their normal food early in the morning, they could only eat the bread baked from rapidly kneaded dough. Musa led his people out of the city and headed straight for the shores of Red Sea. When the day dawned and the Egyptians saw their city to be devoid of the work force they reported this to the Pharaoh. He could not believe that Musa could achieve this mobilisation so fast. His defiance resurged into a mad rage. He mounted his fastest chariot and, in the company of his swiftest horsemen, chased Musa and his people, and caught up with them at the Red Sea.

Miracles of Musa during Exodus

Musa and his people were sandwitched between the army of the Pharaoh and the Red Sea. The Pharaoh laughed at the situation, and said that the God of Musa was not a very clever strategist, and clearly they were at his mercy. He orderd them to return or be killed on the spot. The faith of Bani Israil wavered, and they started to blame Musa for their plight. Musa prayed for help from Allah and hit the waters of Red Sea which created a dry passage between two walls of water. He ordered his people to quickly cross over to the other side. When they were half way down the path, the Pharaoh descended down the same path, in hot pursuit of the fugitives. However, man's designs are no match to that of Allah. As soon as the last of the fugitives had crossed over to the other side, the waters returned to fill the gap, and drowned the defiant Pharaoh, his army, his swift chariot and all their fast horses. Musa prayed to Allah and thanked Him for His Divine Assistance to him and his people.

Arrival at Mount Sinai

Musa led the large caravan through the hot desert of Sinai and arrived at the foot hills of Mount Sinai. The caravan was extremely short of water. They started to moan and blame Musa for having dragged them from the comfort of their homes into the desert with no water or shelter. Having been exposed to the style of idol worship under Egyptian subjugation for generations, they irked to make idols for worship in the old fasion. Musa scolded them on their absurd desire. He prayed to Allah for help and hit a nearby rock with his staff. A spring of sparkling water gushed out from it. They all drank from the spring and washed themselves and their clothing with the plentiful water.

Musa told his people that he was going up the mountain for a few days and Harun would act as his deputy in his absence. They should consider Harun to be their overlord just as he himself was to them, and that they should be obedient to him just as they were to Musa himself. Having given them these instructions, he left for the heights of Mount Sinai.

Revelation of Torah to Musa

Musa returned to the spot where he had first received his miracles from Allah. He took off his shoes as before and went down into subjugation to The Creator and The Sustainer of the universe. He prayed to Allah for His guidance. He was given the Ten Commandments at this session. Before leaving, he begged Allah to be revealed to him. Allah told him that it would not be possible for him to set his eye on His Divine Radiance. He would shower just a little of this over the mighty mountain so that he may derive his satisfaction. No sooner the communication had ended than a blinding pure white radiance struck the mighty mountain and instantaneously turned it into ashes. Musa lost consciousness from the roar that accompanied the lightening. When he recovered, he went down in total submission and asked forgiveness of Allah.

Having thus received the Torah for his people, Musa came down from the mountain and headed for the camp.

Samry and the Golden Bull

In the absence of Musa from the camp, the Israilites defied Harun. Misguided by Samry, a pagan, they collected their golden jewelery and quickly wrought a golden colt from it, as they had done for the temples of the Pharaoh for years. They said that the God of Musa was no where to be seen, and Musa had abandoned them in the wilderness. They started worshipping the Samry's colt, danced around it in sinful pursuits, and indulged in immoral acts.

When Musa arrived at the camp, he was infuriated to see his people in clear defiance of his specific orders. He was very angry with his brother for letting them indulge in blatent *kufr*. Harun told him that they would not listen to him. Musa admonished Samry and broke and burnt his golden colt. As a punishment, the sinning people were ordained to kill one another for atonement of sin.

Banu Israil demand to see God of Musa

After the commotion settled, the elders in the camp insisted upon meeting with God. Musa told them that no one could see Allah but they were adamant. So Musa took seventy selected elders to Mount Sinai. They were not even close to the mountain when a thundering lightening struck in their path. The entire group of insolent people fell to their knees. Musa begged Allah for their forgiveness, and brought them back to the camp. Here they stayed for many days and Musa and his brother Harun educated the people on the Oneness of Allah, and taught them the method of worship as prescribed in the Torah. They sanctified one tent and dedicated it for worship only. They kept this congregational tent with them for worship until they came back to the land of Kin'an where they built the first permanent *Bait-ul-Muqaddas* (the Holy House).

The Gift of *Mann-o-Salwa*

The caravan had exhausted their food supply in the desert and started grumbling. They again blamed Musa for all their difficulties. In his prayers, Musa begged Allah for their relief. Allah sent the gift of *Mann-o-Salwa* (the heavenly meals consisting of meat and sweets) to feed them. They were happy for a short time but started grumbling about the monotonous diet. Now they wanted the traditional diet of lentils garnished with garlic etc. Musa admonished them for their thanklessness. By this time they had reached Palestine, on the border of Kin'an, where they erected their tents in the desert.

The Promised Land

Kin'an was the land that Allah had promised Musa at the end of their jouney, the land of their forefathers. They could see the land from their high perch in the desert. Musa sent Yusha' bin Nun to gather information. It was here that Maryam, the sister of Musa passed away.

47

Yusha' bin Nun came back and reported that the valley was very fertile with fruit groves and vineyards. The people were very tall and strong. Banu Israil refused to go down to claim the territory and face a strong people in combat.

Musa became very disheartened at the defiance and insolence of the people and prayed to Allah for guidance. Allah ordered Musa to take them back to the desert where they would roam in wretchedness for forty years and they would never see the promised land. Hearing this, they agreed to go down to the valley. However Musa advised them to refrain from doing so since Allah had already decreed their renewed toils in the desert. They would not listen, and a large group from amongst them went up the hills. They were attacked by the inhabitants of the valley and many of them were killed in their attempt to gain control of the valley. They had no recourse but to return to the dersert and aimlessly roam there.

Musa took his people and travelled south. When he arrived at Mount Hoor, Harun, his brother passed away. Musa continued to lead his people for the duration of this suffering.

Yusha' bin Nun assisted Musa in the tasks that were previously carried out by Harun.

Forty Years in the Desert

Musa continued the journeys in the desert for forty years as ordained. During this time many of the older folks, who had originated in Egypt, died, and a new generation of

Banu Israil was raised who believed in Allah and followed orders inscribed in the Torah. They were now eager to carry out the biddings of Allah and seek their destiny in the land of Kin'an, the land of their forefathers.

Return to the Promised Land

Musa led them north once again and camped on the opposite banks of River Jordan. He showed them the promised land which their parents had rejected forty years earlier. He told them that he would not be accompanying them beyond the banks of the river. He left them in the camp in the care of Yusha' bin Nun and went up the hill for his prayers.

The Death of Musa

Musa went up the mountain but never came back. He died there, and nobody found him or his grave.

Musa is known as Moses in the Torah.

References: His story has been told in several forms and contexts in al Qur'an. The relevant Suras are as follows: *Baqarah, Alelmran, Nisaa', Maidah, An'am' Anfaal, Yunus, Hud, Ra'ad, Ibrahim, Nahl, Bani Israil, Kahaf, Maryam, Taha, Anmbiya', Mo'min, Furqan, Shu'ra', Qasas, A'nkaboot, Sajdah, Ahzab, Sa'ffat, Haa meem Sajdah, Dukhan, Mujadelah, Ja'thiyah, Zariyat, Qamar, Tahreem, Ha'qah, Muzammil, Naz'at, Fajar.*

HARUN

Harun was the elder brother of Musa. He was son of Imran. He was appointed by Allah to help his brother Musa in the arduous task of freeing and molding the unruly children of Israil into a nation. He was responsible for carrying out of the rituals of worship as assigned by Musa. His descendants still carry out these rituals in the temples of Bani Israil. He acted as the vicegerent of Musa and accompanied his brother through the desert journeys till he died atop Mount Hoor.

References: He is known as Aaron in Torah and is referred to in al Qur'an along with Musa.

YUSHA' BIN NUN

Yusha' bin Nun carried out the first assignment of Musa on their first arrival at the Promised land. After the death of Harun he accompanied Musa in the desert for forty years and carried out all the assignments that were previously carried out by Harun. When they returned to the banks of Jordan River after their wretched journeys in the desert, Musa appointed him his deputy and went up the mountain for the last time. He never came back.

It was Yusha' bin Nun who led Bani Israil into the city of Yareho (Jericho) and arranged the settlement of the twelve tribes of Bani Israil in the land of Kin'an. It was his responsibility to personally see the burial of the remains of Prophet Yusuf amongst his forefathers in accordance with his will.

He died when all the task of settling the Israilites was accomplished according to the Will of Allah.

Yusha' bin Nun is known as Jashua in the Torah.

References: His name is not mentioned in al Qur'an but is referred to along with the narratives of Musa in Sura *Maidah, Kahaf, Waqeah*.

51

SAMUEL

After gaining hold of the new territory, Banu Israil were governed by the clergy in accordance with the laws laid down by Musa in the Torah. After a while they started to dream about a kingdom of their own, just as other people around them had. Allah appointed Samuel prophet to Banu Israil. Samuel was a descendant from Ephraim (a son of Yusuf).

The people made Taalut (Saul in Torah) their king. However, Taalut was unable to govern the people well, and was not obedient to Samuel. Allah took the kingdom away from Taalut and gave it to Da'ud (David).

References: Samuel is not named in al Qur'an, but a refernce is made in *Sura Baqarah* without his name.

DA'UD

Da'ud (David) was a ninth generation descendant of Yahudah (one of the twelve sons of Ya'qub, known as Judah in Torah). Banu Israil were in war with the Eimaliques, and no one was able to subdue their gigantic king called Jalut (Goliath). Da'ud was still a young lad when he used his sling to kill giant king Jalut (Goliath). He was appointed prophet and king by Allah while Samuel was still alive.

The boundaries of his kingdom expanded during his rule, and he spread the religion of Allah to other territories. He laid the foundations of *Bait-ul Muqaddas* (the Holy Mosque) Allah gave him the Book *Zubur* (Psalms in the Torah), that has poetical rhyme and prophetic wisdom in its words. He lived long and ruled his people wisely and in accordance with the laws of Torah.

References: al Qur'an: Sura *Baqarah, Nisaa', Maidah, An'am, Bani Israil, Anmbiya', Nahl, Saba', Jinn.*

SULAYMAN

Sulayman was one of the sons of Da'ud. Allah appointed him prophet and king after his father and gave him immense wisdom and power over all creation, including the jinns. The stories of his justice are alive to this day. His kingdom expanded as far east as Euphrates river, as far west as Egypt, and as far south as Yamen (known as the kingdem of Saba, or Sheba in the Torah).

The queen of Saba, named Bilqis, was so overwhelmed by the power and wisdom of Sulayman that she gave up her kingdom to become his wife and lived with him and by his side.

He completed the construction of *Bait-ul-Muqaddas* whose foundations were laid by his father.

Sulayman is known as King Solomon in the Torah.

References: al Qur'an may be seen in Sura *Baqarah, Nisaa', An'am, Anmbiya', Nahl, Saba, Jinn.*

AYUB

Ayub (Job) was a descendant of A'mis, the third son of Ishaq. Allah had granted him great wealth and a large family, and he lived in comfort and peace.

Allah wanted to test his steadfastness of faith in plenty and in deprivation. Once lightening struck his live stock and all his animals perished. This was followed by a storm that destroyed his crops. The test of deprivation continued, and his house collapsed over his family, killing all his children. Every time a calamity struck, he went down in submission to Allah acknowledging that *the Lord giveth and the Lord taketh away.* There is none other than Allah who has the power to provide and sustain His creatures in this world and beyond.

The trial of patience continued, and Ayub developed ulcers over all his body, and the maggots ate his rotting flesh. At these troubled times, many of his friends and followers abandoned him. Only his beloved wife Raheemah stayed with him throughout his troubles. She washed and caressed his wounds and fed him with whatever she could gather.

The towns people forced him and his devoted wife out into the wilderness. The series of painful trials did not shake him in his belief in the Benevolence of Allah. He exhibited his contentment over the trials of life and with whatever meager provisions he had. Allah was pleased with His steadfast servant. He gave him full recovery from his oozing sores. Upon recovery from his illness, he toiled in his land and regained his wealth that far exceeded his previous possessions. Allah granted him new and expanded progeny. His circle of friends and followers grew larger than ever, and all wonderd over what Ayub had sustained. This added greater strength to the faith of the believers.

The patience and perseverence of Ayub in the face of all suffering is proverbial and the best example for people of all times.

<u>References:</u> al Qu'an: Sura *An'am, Anmbiya', Jinn.*

ILYAS

Ilyas was a descendant from the progeny of Harun and was a great prophet of Allah amongst Banu Insrail.

The king of Bani Israil had reverted to materialism. He was married to a heathen woman. Banu Israil followed their king and carved out several stone idols for worship including the calf that was a popular god amongst the Phillistines. Any one who stood up for the monotheistic faith of Musa was slain ruthlessly. This was the time when many prophets of Allah were martyred because they taught the truth and wanted people to return to the religion of Allah.

The king and his queen had their neighbor killed because he was a man of pious conduct and of monotheistic faith; and annexed his fertile fruit groves to their own. Ilyas rebuked them for their ill conduct. He told them that if they did not repent on what they had wrought against an innocent family, return the groves to the orphan of the slain owner, Allah will send his punishment upon them, and they will be similarly slain in the same fruit garden. The king told Ilyas that he should refrain from confrontation with him or else he will have him arrested and tortured for his harsh words against his king.

It so happened that the young son of the king became ill. Ilyas asked the king why did he not pray to his best idol for the recovery of his son. The king was so annoyed with the harsh words of Ilyas that he sent his palace guards to arrest him and bring him into his presence so that he could be tortured and killed in his presence. Ilyas prayed to Allah for His help. The palace guards fell down dead, and Ilyas was spared.

Allah sent his punishment for the people in the form of a drought. Ilyas challenged them to go and sing and dance to please their false gods and see if they would send some rain for them. Clearly all the elements are subservient to Allah and no amount of material power can match His Will. They did all that was known to them but nothing happened.

When hearts harden with hate and defiance, no amount of logic or reason makes any sense. They all swooped on Ilyas to lynch him in public. They blamed him for his magic to be the cause of their misery. They conspired to kill him.

Ilyas appointed Al-Yasa' his successor and vanished in the protection of Allah. A monarch from a neighboring kingdom came and conquered the land. The king and his queen met their ill fate as predicted by Ilyas, and were slain in the same grove where they had killed its innocent owner. Their bodies lay rotting in the sun, and ravens and vultures ate their flesh.

References: al Qur'an: *Sura Sa'ffat.*

ZULKIFL

Zulkifl was a contemporary of Ilyas. He was a very pious man of Allah and was well respected by the people. He was responsible for saving lives of over a hundred prophets and men of Allah during the rule of an Israilite king and his heathen wife who would kill any one opposing their practice of idolatory.

He is named Zulkifl in al Qur'an , which means the savior or protector. He is named Abadihah in the Torah.

References: al Qur'an: *Sura Anmbiya', Jinn.*

AL-YASA'

Al-Yasa' was the son of Safet and was appointed his *khalifa* by Ilyas before he vanished into the protection of Allah. He was appointed prophet to Banu Israil after Ilyas.

He inherited from Ilyas the obstinate king and queen of Bani Israil who would not listen to any reason. Al-Yasa' did many miraculous deeds to show them the powers of Allah but they called him a magician like they had called Ilyas before him. They continued defying throughout his life.

After a period of time the mighty Assyrians conquered Bani Israil, destroyed their dwellings including the *Bait-ul Muqqadas* and took away all the precious relics. They raged such havoc in the land that several tribes of Bani Israil have lost their ancestoral traces to this day.

References: al Qur'an: *Sura An'am, Jinn*.

YUNUS

Yunus son of Amittai in the clan of Judah was appointed prophet by Allah towards the people of Ninewah (North Western Iraq). The people were very head strong and obstinate. They refused to listen to his teachings. He got disgusted and disappointed with the lack of progress with the people. He prayed to Allah to punish the people for defying him, and decided to take the river ferry to go to another territory.

While crossing the river, great swells engulfed the ferry. When it appeared that the boat would sink with the next swell, the captain of the boat addressed the passengers and said that there must be someone amongst them who had run away from his master. He should give himself up and come forward so that he may be tossed overboard to save the rest. No one moved for a while. When the next swell struck the boat, and it was evident that the end was near, they decided to toss a coin and it fell for Yunus. So he was thrown in the river. The storm subsided immediately and all on board the ferry were saved.

As for Yunus, a large fish swallowed him and carried him to the banks of the river where he was ejected on to dry land. His skin got eroded from the digestive juices of the fish. He suffered great pain and disappointment because of the flies and the sun. He sought forgiveness from Allah for having abandoned his mission. Allah made a plant come up by his side and he convalasced under its shadow by the river bank, and reflected over the extra-ordinary experience.

61

In the meantime, his people had realized their error. They repented for their sin and ventured out in search of Yunus. They found him and rejoiced seeing him alive. They took him back and promised to live by his teachings. He lived amongst his people to a long and ripe age. When he died, he was buried near the same place where the great fish had ejected him. Many devout followers started to build their homes at this location and it soon developed into a bustling city. The city of Kufa is located at the same historic site and the grave of Prophet Yunus is located at the bank of the river.

Yunus is also known as Zunnun since he had emerged from the stomach of a fish.

References: al Qur'an: *Sura Nisaa', An'am, Yunus, Anmbiya', Sa'ffat, Qalam.*

UZAIR

The Babylonian king Nabukatnazar (Bakht Nasr) ransacked the dwellings of Bani Israil and their dead bodies lay decaying in the desert sun. Uzair was grieved at the total annihilation and wondered how could the lost glory of the cities of Bani Israil be ever revived again. A sudden slumber came upon him and he remained in that state for one hundred years.

Then Allah made him rise from his sleep. When he got up, he looked at his donkey. He was surprized to see only the bones of its decaying skeleton. He wondered what had happened to his donkey. He then noted that his food was as fresh as it was when he fell asleep. He was wondering about all this when Allah asked him if he knew how long he had been asleep. He said, " for a day, or even less!" Allah then told him that he had slept for a hundred years. During this period, his perishables remained fresh by His permission, but his living animal had undergone the natural process of death and dissolution. Then Allah made his donkey also come to life in front of his eyes. Uzair acknowledged that Allah had total command over all things.

He then headed for the "ruins" of the dwellings he had seen before his "sleep" and saw that the cities had been totally rebuilt and life was bustling again. He was received by the king with great curiosity and when they heard his strange story, they said he had to be the Son of God, to have

63

come back from amongst the dead! In Qur'an, Allah has admonished Bani Israil who had this false belief.

He is known as Ezra in Torah.

References: al Qur'an: *Sura Baqarah, Taubah.*

LUQMAN

Luqman was a great wise man of Allah. He is famous for laying down the principles of high quality of human conduct and wisdom.

His Great Personal Conduct

He believed in the Oneness of Allah and obeyed His commandment with honesty and commitment. He was a great observer and thinker. He avoided sleeping during the day, and would not sit back in comfortable posture when he had company. He was so mannerly that no one ever saw him spitting. He avoided joking, and laughing lest it would displease Allah. He neither rejoiced over achieving something nor grieved over losing it. He always helped to settle differences between parties. He prefered to sit amongst gatherings of the wise and remained silent unless spoken to. He carefully watched the conduct of the rulers.

Allah had bestowed upon him the gift of wisdom and insight about the affairs of people. Allah ordained him to be always thankful, for "Whosoever denies His blessings does so only to his own peril."

He gave an eternal guidance to humanity in the form of advice to his son which is stated in Qur'an.

On The Great Sin of Polytheism

"O son, be careful, never associate any one with Allah because it is a grave sin and there is no forgiveness for it."

On Thankfulness to Allah for His Benevolence, and On The Rights of Parents, and Their Obedience

"O son, be humble and charitable towards your parents. Thank Allah first for all that He has granted you without your asking for it, and then thank your parents for the kindness they showed you, when you were helpless.

"If the parent are polytheistic and force you to follow them in their faith, do not obey them in this respect, but without causing any harm to them. Continue to serve them with good conduct. Be kind to them even if they are wrong.

Careful and Cautious Conduct

He continued his advice: "O son, Your deeds , good or bad, and in any amount, are accountable on the Great Day of Reckoning. Your reward or punishment will depend on the quality of your conduct.

"Do not slumber when you should be awake and stand in worship of your Lord. Learn to bear in the times of deprivation, for Allah rewards those who show contentment and forbearance.

66

"Do not exhibit arrogance as you walk or talk, as Allah does not consider arrogance to be an appropriate behavior amongst human beings.

"Show moderation in your attire and adornments.

"Talk in low tone, because the loud and the crude tone belongs to the ass."

References: alQur'an: *Sura Luqman.*

ZAKARIYA

Zakariya was a prophet amongst Banu Israil and was the father of Yahya. He was responsible for the rituals of worship as well as the upkeep of *Bait-ul Muqqadas*.

Fostering care of Maryam

Maryam was a niece of his wife. The mother of Maryam had dedicated her unborn child to serve *Bait-ul Muqqadas*. When she gave birth to a daughter, she did not retract from her vow of dedicating her child in the service of *Bait-ul Muqqadas* and gave her to the foster care of her uncle, Zakariya.

When she grew up, he started to take her along to the great Mosque and taught her how to take care of all the sacred objects and how to conduct the rituals of worship. When she grew older, he alloted her a room inside the Mosque so that she could carry out her duties independently, and at all times.

The Birth of Yahya

Zakariya had grown old and his wife was infertile. Allah revealed to him that he would have a son very soon who would be a great prophet and a leader. His conduct would be exemplary to all mankind. There had never been any one before him with the same name, and that his name would be Yahya. He would affirm the innocence of Maryam. Zakariya was struck with amazement over the possibility of having a child at his old age and through his wife who had been infertile all her life. Allah conveyed to him that there is nothing that is impossible for Him to do. Allah gave Zakariya His sign for the prophecy, that he would be incapable of verbal communication with any one for a period of three days. So Zakariya was unable to talk for three days as the angel of Allah had forewarned him. Soon afterwards he had the son whom he named Yahya, according to the Will of Allah.

He is known as Zacharia in the Torah.

References: al Qur'an: *Sura Ale Imran, An'am, Maryam, Anmbiya'*.

YAHYA

Yahya was born during the reign of king Harrod who was a puppet monarch under the rulers of Rome. He was the son that Allah had promised to Zakariya in his old age. There had never been any one before him with that name. He had shown compassion to serve mankind right from his childhood. As he grew older, his conduct in the society was cosidered exemplary. He was kind hearted towards others, and was obedient to his parents and elders. He lived strictly according to the Torah and urged others to follow it for their salvation. He gave baptismal rites to all those who listened to his call.

When Bani Israil laid blame on Maryam over the virgin birth of Isa, he bore witness of her piety and innocence. He affirmed the prophethood of Isa when he was appointed to his mission by Allah.

The Roman rulers disapproved the activities of Yahya and got him killed through the king Harrod.

He is known in the Bible as John the Baptist.

References: al Qur'an in: Sura *Ale Imran, An'am, Mariyam, Anmbiya'*.

ISA

Isa was the last prophet appointed by Allah for Bani Israil. They defied his teachings and denied his legitimacy. In collaboration with the Roman governor of Palestine, the Jews had him framed for treason, that was punishable by crucifixion. However Allah saved him from death by crusifixion. His teachings were adapted by other subjects of the Roman empire which laid the foundations of Christianity.

The Birth of Isa

Maryam, the mother of Isa was dedicated in the service of *Bait-ul Muqqadas* and used to live in a cubicle assigned to her for her residence. One day an angel of Allah appeared to her in her cubicle and told her that Allah had willed that she be the mother of a great prophet. Maryam was frightened at seeing the angel in front of her in the form of a young man, and more so on learning that she would be a mother without ever having been married. The angel told her not to be afraid and to trust in Allah. He is the Creator of all things, and has ways and means of creating any thing whenever He wills.

When Maryam found herself to be pregnant, she left her cubicle in the grand mosque and made her way into the desert. Isa was born in the solitude of the desert. The new mother sat under a palm tree with ber baby son, feeling distraught and dejected at her predicament. The angel

71

appeared to her again and told her that she should not feel so low at her present condition, for Allah is the greatest Provider and Sustainer. He told her to shake the palm tree and enough dates would fall in her lap for her sustenance, and she could drink fresh water from a spring that came out by her side. The angel also told her, " When the people ask you about the baby, say nothing; point towards him and he will bear witness to the Will of Allah and he will talk on her behalf."

The Miraculous Speech by the Infant Isa

As Maryam returned to *Bait-ul Muqqadas,* the rabbi blocked her way saying that she had no room in the place of worship. When she turned around, a crowd had gathered around her. Curious and agitated, they wanted to know who was the father of the baby. She did as instructed by Allah, and pointed towards the infant. They all laughed at this and said how could a new born answer their questions. However, Isa spoke up with the permission of Allah and said, "I am a servant of Allah. He has appointed me as prophet amongst you and am the bearer of the Book (Injeel). Allah has granted me bounties of benevolence and made me obedient to my mother. I will worship Allah and obey all His laws for as long as I live." He became quiet after that. The people were dumb founded at this miracle and they dispersed. The stories of this supernatural event remained in circulation for a long time.

The controversies over the Virgin Birth of Isa

The Jews consider Isa to be an illegitimate child of Maryam. The Christians consider him the son of God. Allah says He is neither a husband nor a father. He is the Creator and Sustainer of all things. He settled the controversy over the birth of Isa in al Qur'an: " Verily, for Allah the circumstances over the birth of Isa are no different from those surrounding the origin of Adam. He created Adam from no parents at all, while Isa had a mother. He just has to will some thing to happen, and it materializes at once. He would raise the dead from their graves on the Day of Judgement by His Divine Will, for He is All Powerful and Magnificient."

The Prophethood of Isa and his Miracles

Isa was thirty years of age when he began to receive Divine Revelations and started to teach Banu Israil the commandments of Allah. He showed them great miracles that indicated the grandeur of Allah. He made birds from the mud and made them fly. He healed the leppers, he gave vision to the blind, he brought back life to the dead and fed thousands from a mere loaf of bread, all with the permission of Allah. He confirmed the truth of Torah and affirmed the ordinances of *halal (permitted) and haram (prohibited)* and revised certain canonical laws to suit the circumstances of that society. He called upon the rabbis of *Bait-ul Muqqadas* to clear it from all trading activities and clean it up for the worship of Allah. He met with the stubborn antagonism from his people except for a handful of true believers. He had twelve disciples, or companions (also known as the twelve apostles of Jesus) who followed him wherever he went and assisted him in his teachings.

Bani Israil did not approve the teachings of Isa and collaborated with the Roman governor of the land to get rid of him.

The Occultation of Isa

One of the companions of Isa betrayed him and handed him over to the government agents who were seeking to arrest Isa for treason. The Roman governor and Banu Israil believed that they had crucified Isa. Some of his followers thought that he was taken down from the cross before he actually died on the cross. The controversy still continues. Allah clarifies this in al Qur'an that it is a waste of time even to conjecture on the nature of Isa or what happened to him after his arrest by the Romans. He was niether crusified nor did he die on the cross. Allah withdrew him from amongst his blood thirsty enemies and raised him to the heaven.

References : al Qur'an: *Sura AleImran, Nisaa', Maidah, An'am, Mariyam, Anmbiya', Momenun, Zakhraf, Hadeed, Saa Faa, Tahreem.*

MUHAMMAD

The Last Prophet of Allah

Allah proclaimed Muhammad as the last prophet. In the Qur'an, he is called *"Rahmatun-lil-aalameen,"* the blessing for the universe.

Names of Muhammad

The Prophet of Islam has many popular names. He was named Muhammad at birth. Other names include Ahmad, Taha, Yaseen, Muzammil, Mustafa, Rahmatun-lil-aalameen, Khairul Mursaleen and Khatamun Nabiyyeen. His Kunniyya include Abul Qasim and Abu Ibrahim.

The Genealogy of Muhammad

The genealogy of Muhammad can be traced eighteen generations back to *Abul A'arab* Ismail, son of Ibrahim. His father Abdullah was one of the ten sons of Abd al-Muttaleb bin Hashim, the highly respected chief in the clan of Quraysh. His mother Amenah, daughter of Wahb, belonged to the respected clan of Banu Zuhra in the clan of Quraysh.

The Birth and early life of Muhammad

According to the popular tradition, Muhammad was born in Makkah (Mecca) on Friday, 17 Rabi-ul Awwal in the year of the Elephant *(Am al Feel)*, or August 29, 570 AD. Muhammad's father had died a few months before his birth. His grand-father, Abd al-Muttaleb took him under his own foster care.

According to the custom of Quraysh, the women from modest tribes living in the desert around Makkah were engaged for wages to suckle the new born babies. These were sought for the infant Muhammad. After trying no less than eight prospective nurses, the grand son of Abd al-Muttaleb felt comfortable in the lap of Haleemah, a magnificent lady from the tribe of Banu S'ad. He stayed with Haleemah in the desert upto the age of about four (or six) years.

When he was returned to the full care of his own mother, she took him to her ancestoral city, Yathreb (later renamed Madinah), to introduce him to the people of his maternal clan. On their way, she died in the village of Abwa', between Madinah and Makkah, and she was buried there. Muhammad was brought back to the care of his grand father.

Muhammad was only eight years old when his grand father, Abd al-Muttaleb also died. At this time, his uncle Abu Talib (father of Ali) took his orphan nephew in his personal care. He grew up under the most affectionate guardianship of Abu Talib and his wife Fatimah binte Asad. They always treated him like one of their own sons.

Observations on the early life of Muhammad

Muhammad grew to his youth in the house of Abu Talib, who adored his nephew for his good nature and style.

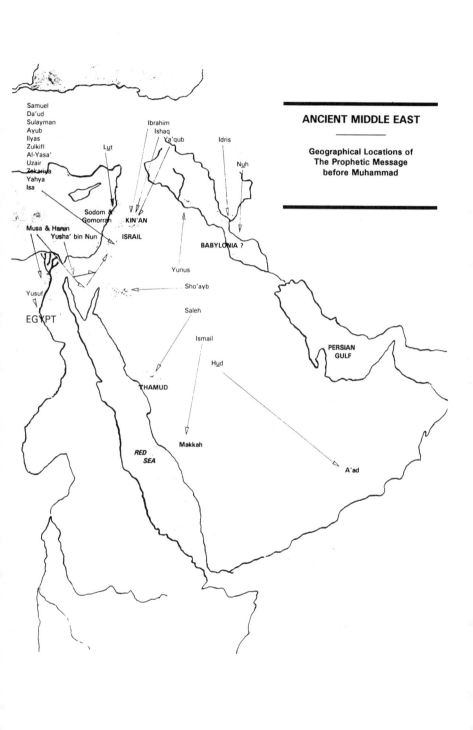

ANCIENT MIDDLE EAST

Geographical Locations of
The Prophetic Message
before Muhammad

Samuel
Da'ud
Sulayman
Ayub
Ilyas
Zulkifl
Al-Yasa'
Uzair
Zekariya
Yahya
Isa

Ibrahim
Ishaq
Ya'qub

Idris

Lut

Nuh

Sodom &
Gomorrah   KIN'AN

Musa & Harun
Yusha' bin Nun   ISRAIL

BABYLONIA ?

Yunus

Yusuf

Sho'ayb

EGYPT

Saleh

Ismail

PERSIAN
GULF

Hud

THAMUD

Makkah

RED
SEA

A'ad

He loved him more than his own children. Abu Talib made many observations on the habits of Muhammad. Some of these are quoted below:

Whenever Muhammad had a meal, he always started by saying "*Bismillah*....i.e. I begin with the name of Allah, and finished by saying *Alhamdu lillah*....i.e. all praise to Allah." He said that they were so touched by this fine habit of Muhammad that the whole family adopted his manner.

Abu Talib noted Muhammad saying his prayers in a way not known to him before. He asked his nephew to explain to him the method of his worship. When he heard the reasons for the rituals, he was so pleased that he urged his sons to join Muhammad in his ritual worship.

It is quoted from Abu Talib that Muhammad never told lies nor fabricated events. He did not waste his time nor indulged in unproductive activities. He liked solitude, and devoted some of his time for meditation. He spoke to others with courtesy and respect. He was so honest in his dealings that he became known as "Al Ameen" (the most honest and trustworthy person).

Trips to Syria with Abu Talib

Muhammad accompanied his uncle twice on trading trips to the city of Damascus, in the then Roman province of Syria.

Many traditions are quoted by several authors regarding these trips. On the first trip he was only thirteen years of age. A Christian monk named Bahera

PROGENY OF IBRAHIM

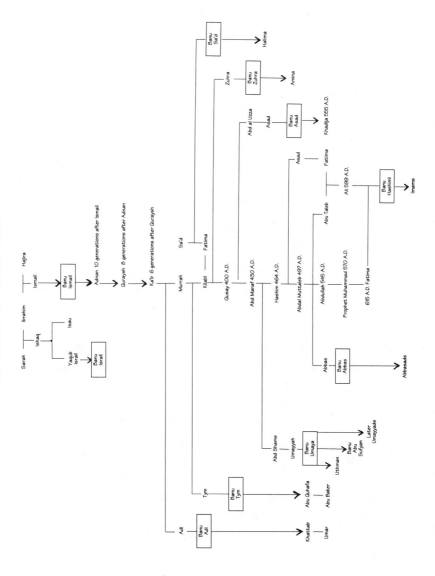

observed Muhammad closely and cautiond Abu Talib to take particular care of the youth, for he saw signs of greatness in him. On the second trip, now fully grown to manhood, he met the same monk again. This time Bahera told Abu Talib that he saw signs of prophethood in his nephew and that he should protect him from harm.

Trips to Syria in the employment of Khadija

Khadija was a wealthy busineswoman who used to send out reputable traders to Syria to conduct trading business on her behalf. She was a very kind hearted lady who spent a lot of her wealth on social services amongst her tribe. One of her widowed cousins named Hala lived in her household with her three daughters, and she brought up these girls after her death.

Abu Talib wanted to introduce his favourite nephew Muhammad into an independent trade. At the same time, Khadija had heard about the honesty of Abu Talib's nephew. On the recommendation of Abu Talib, she gave an appointment to Muhammd to lead her trade caravan to Syria. During this trip, he was accompanied by Khadija's personal servant, Maisarah.

On this trip, they came across another monk called Nestorah who also affirmed the previous predictions of Baherah. The trading went exceptionally well and they made unusual profit in their transactions. They returned home laiden with exchanged merchandise. Khadija was very pleased at the great success of her trading mission under Muhammad and wondered over the stories her servant had told her about him.

Marriage to Khadija and their progeny

Muhammad had reached marriageable age of twenty five years. Khadija was forty. The proposal of marriage for the two, originating from Khadija, was gladly accepted by Muhammad, after consultation with his uncle, and they were married. The *nikah* was recited by Abu Talib. They had three sons and one daughter from this marriage, but only the daughter Fatima survived. Her brothers Qasim, Abdullah and Taher (Tayyeb) all died in infancy.

The Cave of Hira and the beginnings of Divine Revelations

Muhammad regularly visited a cave known as Hira, high in one of the mountains surrounding Makkah. He meditated and pondered over the complications and intricacies of the creation. During one of these days when he was deep in thought, the archangel Jibril of Allah appeared in front of him and asked him to read. Muhammad asked him what was he to read, for he had not received any formal education. Jibril told him again " Read in the name of Allah who created man from but a mere clot. It is only He whom you must trust. It is He who teaches every thing. He is who teaches all that can be inscribed, and it is He who taught man what he knew not. "

After this extra-ordinary experience in the cave, Muhammad returned home and narrated this to his wife Khadija. She at once remembered the predictions that had been made about the prophethood of her husband. She comforted him and he laid down under the cover of a light blanket.

Jibril came down to him again with the message of Allah, "O, you who is lying under cover of the blanket, this is no time to rest! Get up and spread the message with energy and diligence!" This was a formal mandate to him to proclaim his prophethood.

According to some reports, his daughter, Fatima was born in the same year.

The Methods of Spreading the Message

The task was tough. The people were totally immersed in idolatory. Many of them were rich and arrogant. He wondered how would he approach them and commence his task. Allah sent Jibril again and advised him not to despair for He would provide him with guidance and systematic instructions on how to begin the mission of spreading His message:

i	Start with your closest relatives
ii	For those who accept your teachings, show kindness and forbearance and encourage them towards compliance
iii	For those who defy you, just tell them that you had delivered the message of the Creator, and that from then on you exonerate yourself from their deeds
iv	Do not despair. Trust in Allah. He will help you in your task. Be confident that your sustenance and support for this mission comes only from your Provider, Allah.

The First Muslims

Encouraged by these clear instructions from Allah the Prophet of Islam, Muhammad started his mission by calling his relatives to a banquet on two separate occasions. He announced his prophethood as ordained by Allah. They ridiculed him and did not accept his message. His beloved wife Khadija gave him support and consolation at these frustrating moments and became the first one to accept him as the messenger of Allah. She laid down her entire wealth and personal resources in the service of Islam.

His nephew Ali, whom he had nurtured from infancy, was the first youth of Makkah to accept the prophethood of Muhammad. In fact he stood up at each of the banquets boldly and confirmed the prophethood of Muhammad.

Zaid bin Harith, a youth fostered by Muhammad, known in some traditions as his adopted son was also one of the first to accept Islam.

Abu Bakar was the first amongst the elders to join the small group of the early muslims.

General Call to join the Truth

Undaunted by the hostile response from his clansmen and other Makkans, the Prophet went to the holy precinct of the Ka'ba to make his announcement. He called upon the people to abandon worship of false gods and idols and return to the Creator, the All Powerfull Allah. He said that if they would join him in his call, Allah would make them a very respected community and grant them power and control over vast lands beyond their own. People initially laughed at such prospect. Their hearts were hardened. They did not want to give up the worship of their popular gods that had been handed down to them for generations. Later, they became more hostile to Muhammad and his followers.

Hostilities of the Kuffar against the Muslims

The arrogant and rich elite of Makkah subjected the early muslims to painful torture which killed some of them and maimed others. The steadfast believers did not waver in their belief.

Having failed to achieve their ends through the use of force, the pagan Arabs sent a delegation to Abu Talib to protest agaist Muhammad and his teachings. They told him that they were prepared to pay Muhammad any amount of money he wanted, or he could marry any beautiful woman he chose, and they would even accept him as the Chief of Makkah if he stopped talking against their idols. Muhammad refused their offers and said that the mission on which he had embarked, could not be bought or bribed with any amount of worldly riches.

They turned to Abu Talib and offered Ghamaza bin Walid in exchange for Muhammad, but he refused the absurd exchange. He said that he would never surrender his nephew to them for any reason. He asked Muhammad to continue doing what he must, and that he would always support him.

First Hijra to Abyssenia

Muhammad was into his fifth year of teaching while his followers continued to suffer untold tortures at the hands of kuffar. He ordered his followers to leave the hostilities of the kuffar and take refuge in the Christian kingdom of Abyssenia under king Negus. There were only eleven men and four women among the first migrants to Abyssenia. Uthman and his wife Ruqayya were also amongst this group of believers.

Second Hijra to Abyssenia

Only a short while later, a second group of eighty two muslims were instructed to migrate to Abyssenia. The group was led by Ja'far bin Abu Talib. The kuffar were enraged at the escape of their fugitives to the neigboring kingdom across the Red Sea. They sent their representation to King Negus, along with presents and gifts, and asked the extradition of their fugitives.

The Address by Ja'ffar bin Abu Talib and the recitation of al Qur'an in the court of King Negus

The kuffar alleged that the fugitives rebuked their gods and idols, and were disrupting the practice of their old religion. King Negus was a Christian and did not believe in idolatory. So he was not prepared to release the fugitives on that ground. The kuffar then lied that the Muslims said unkind words about Isa and his mother Maryam. At this allegation, the king asked the leader of the fugitives to come forward and answer the allegations. Ja'ffar bin Abu Talib got up and addressed the king and his court thus:

83

" O king, we were a people sunken deep in ignorance. We had abandoned the teachings of our fore fathers Ibahim and Ismail. We worshiped idols and false gods, indulged in base activities without shame or remorse. We had lost affection for the very young and showed no compassion for the aged or infirm, and killed our female infants. Allah has sent us a prophet whose truthfulness is acknowledged even by his foes. He comes from a pure family and teaches us things that make us respect life and the bounties of the Creator. He tells us to believe in one God only, and not split Him or attribute partners with Him. He tells us to deal with others with honesty, not usurp others' rights, love children and respect elders. He has taught us to handle our women with love and respect, and give them the rights that they deserve as mothers, wives, daughters or sisters. He forbade us to kill our daughters as their provision comes from the Divine Sustainer of all creation.

"We decided to follow him in what he has taught us. We have stolen nothing, nor are we fugitives of war. He told us to flee from oppression into your protection.

"As for the allegations regarding Isa, the Qur'an has a chapter regarding the events of his birth and prophethood."

He then recited a few *ayat* (verses) from Sura Maryam. The style and melody of his recitation, and the truth and the contents of the *ayat* had a profound effect on the king and his courtiers. Their hearts moved and their eyes were moistened with tears.

The king announced that the immigrants were not to be treated as fugitives in his country but as their respected guests. They could live as they pleased and trade in peace under his protection. He told the pursuers to leave his country and never come again seeking extradition of the Muslims.

The Declaration of Faith by Hamza and Umar

The unsuccessful return of the envoy from Abyssenia further fueled hostilities against Muhammad and his followers. One day Hamza bin Abd al-Muttaleb came to know that the kuffar had stoned the Prophet and had thrown garbage over him during his prayer. He came storming to the scene, beat up the infidel crowd until they ran for their lives. Hamza recited the *kalima* in public and joined the group of the believers.

Umar bin Khattab was short tempered by nature. One day he heard his sister reciting from al Qur'an. He admonished her, and in a rage, rushed to the place where the Prophet was addressing the Muslims. On hearing the Prophet recite the *ayas* of Qur'an, his anger melted away, and he accepted Islam by reciting the *kalima.*

The Muslims seek shelter in She'be Abi Talib

Islam was making steady progress, to great frustration of the *kuffar*. Their opposition to the Prophet reached its peak. Abu Sufyan spearheaded the move to boycott Muhammad and his followers and forced them and their Hashimite supporters to take shelter in a fortress known as She'be Abi Talib. The blockade included total boycott of the Muslims and the Hashimites from all social and economic activities. The agreement was written and unanimously signed by all the chiefs of the *kuffar* clans of Makkah in 616 AD. The *kuffar* enforced a ban and excommunication against the inmates of She'b̲e Abi Talib. Abu Sufyan also had personal motives to get the leadership of Makkah transferred from the house of Hashim to his own. The *kuffar* demanded from Abu Taleb to either surrender unconditionally, or to hand over to them Muhammad and his followers. Abu Talib refused their demands and suffered the blockade along with the Muslims. He suffered a considerable financial and social set-back due to the blockade. The Muslims remained steadfast in their beliefs, and continued their practice of Islam under the protection of Abu Talib.

Abu Talib wrote a beautiful eulogy about his nephew, the Prophet of Islam. It is a written testimony of his love for the Prophet and his mission. The *kuffar* got tired of the three year long blockade and had no choice but to lift it completely. The Muslims returned to their homes once again and resumed their social interactions with the other towns people.

The Year of Grief

It was only two months after the lifting of the blockade, that Abu Talib passed away. He had fostered Muhammad as his own son, introduced him to trading, and got him married. He protected and defended him against the *kuffar*. He declared his faith in Islam before he died. He was a respected elder of the community and was able to serve Islam in its early days. He was a true ally of the small community of early Muslims. He provided them support and shelter in their hardship. His death was indeed a great loss to Muhammad and his friends.

To further grief of the Prophet, only three days after the death of his beloved uncle, his devoted wife Khadija also died. Khadija was not only the first of the believers but also a comforter of the Prophet in his difficult days. She was a great sustainer and benefactor of the early muslims. Her death was a painful loss for Muhammad as well as his followers.

This year was named by the prophet as *Aamm-ul-Huzn* (the year of grief) because of these two deaths.

Visit to Taif

The Prophet had lost his two best supporters. The Makkan's enemosity reached its highest peak and they increased their atrocities against the Prophet and his followers.

The Prophet of Allah decided to take his mission to Taif, a town about seventy miles east of Makkah. He called upon the people to stop bowing to false gods and idols and return to the worship of Allah, the one and only Lord and Sustainer of the Universe. He was not received well in the town. The people threw stones at him. Bruised and bleeding, he left Taif.

Heart broken and disappointed at the response of the people of Taif, the Prophet returned to Makkah. He was received with ridicule and opposition, but he continued his mission in an undaunted and resolute manner.

By now, the news of the teachings of Muhammad had also reached the people of Yathreb (later renamed Madinah, or Medina)

Spreading the Message to Yathreb

Six men from the tribe of Khazraj (in Yathreb) were visiting Makkah. They met with the Prophet and accepted Islam. They returned to their homes with new enlightenment. The following year twelve more people from the Banu Khazraj visited the Prophet and joined the group of believers. Upon their return, the Prophet sent one of his companions to further the cause of Islam in Yathreb. The next year more people from Banu Khazraj as well as Banu Aws visited the Prophet and accepted Islam as their way of life. Upon their returning home, they extended invitation to the Prophet and his followers to emigrate to Yathreb so that other members of their tribes could benefit from his teachings.

Al-Isra'- A Unique Miracle

Just before the Prophet had migrated to Yathreb, Allah took him on a miraculous ascension to the Heavens, known as al-Isra'(or al-Me'raj). One night while he was resting in the house of his cousin Umm-e-Hani, he was transported to the mosque, al-Aqsa *(Bait-ul-Muqqadis)* in Jerusalem. After he had offered his prayers, he was taken on a miraculous tour of the skies and worlds beyond. The divine vehicle used for his flight is known as *Burraq* which can be translated "as fast as *burq* (lightening)." This exta-terrestrial experience was in body, not in soul. By al-Isra', Allah had intended for Muhammad to see the span and the vastness of His universe and secrets of the heavens. After all, unlike other prophets, his prophethood encompassed the whole universe. The Prophet returned to pursue his task with a renewed vigor.

Some people consider al-Me'raj as a spiritual, not bodily experience. They lose sight of the infinite powers of Allah and other reported miracles of the Prophets Ibrahim, Idris, Ilyas, Musa and Isa. There is nothing difficult for Allah. Al-Me'raj of the Prophet of Islam was truly a precursor of the modern day man's flight in space.

Hijra

The Prophet and his followers had to suffer at the hands of kuffar of Makkah for fourteen years until he told his followers to start emigrating to Yathreb. The move was to be slow and casual so that the kuffar would not cause trouble or block it. In the meantime he remained in Makkah to continue his mission and supervise the slow emigration of his followers. The few people left in Makkah beside himself included his daughter Fatima, his cousin Ali, Ali's mother Fatima binte Asad and his friend Abu Bakar. The time for their migration had now come. He assigned Ali to stay back, and sleep in his bed. He asked him to distribute all the goods to the people who had deposited these with him for safe keeping. Accompanied by Abu Bakar, the Prophet left Makkah in the darkness of night.

In the meanwhile, the *kuffar* patrolled the streets around the house of Muhammad and looked over the low walls of his courtyard. They saw nothing and suspected no movement in the house through the night. As the day dawned, they broke into the house. They were enraged to see Ali on the bed instead of Muhammad. They angrily asked Ali regarding the whereabouts of Muhammad. Ali asked them if they had left him in his custody. They were embarrassed by this clever answer and left the house in search of the Prophet.

89

Ali carried out the instructions of the Prophet and hastened to join him at Quba, on the way to Yathreb.

The Cave of Thaur and the Miracles of Allah

The Prophet and his companion, Abu Bakar took refuge in the cave of Thaur, just outside the city of Makkah. The kuffar were not about to give up their search for the escapees. Their search brought them to this cave. Upon hearing the footsteps of the pursuers, Abu Bakar showed fear for their being discovered in the cave. The Prophet told him not to be scared because Allah was with them. Just then a spider spun a web at the entrance of the cave, and a dove laid eggs over a nest. Hence the *kuffar* did not suspect there was any body in the cave. They left to continue their search elsewhere.

The Prophet and his companion stayed in the cave for three days. When the danger had subsided, they made their way towards Yathreb.

Arrival at Yathreb

The Prophet approached the city of Yathreb on 12 Rabi ul-Awwal, according to 2 July, 622AD and made his first stop at Quba. Ali joined them at this location, and the caravan proceeded towards the city. A Mosque was subsequently built at Quba and exists to this day.

The people of Yathreb who had been receiving muslim refugees from Makkah were anxiously waiting for the arrival of the Prophet himself. Everybody wanted the Prophet to stay in his house. The Prophet took a unique precaution so that no body would feel left out. He freed the reins of his camel and said that the camel would stop wherever Allah wanted it. Finally the camel sat down in front of the house of Abu Ayyub Ansari. The Prophet stayed with this family until his own quarters were ready. The city of Yathreb became popularly known as *Madina-tun-Nabi* i.e. the city of the Prophet, and later as Madinah (or Medina).

Building of Masjid-un-Nabi

The Prophet bought an empty lot from the owner and built the Grand Mosque at that site. It was not grand because of the beautiful construction but because it was built by the Prophet for the first grand congregation of muslims. The Prophet and his family built their quarters around this mosque, as did some of his companions too.

Initiation of the Brotherhood of Islam

As a fairly large number of refugees had come to Madinah, mostly without their belongings, it was necessary to provide for their needs as well as integrate them with the host community. It was for this reason that the Prophet initiated at a simple ceremony, what is called the *Akhuwwa* or Brotherhood among his followers. According to this, each Medinite was named to be brother of a refugee from Makkah, and like real brothers, they now would equally own their businesses or properties. It was in the same year that Salman Farsi and Abdallah bin Salman, a Jew, visited the Prophet and accepted Islam.

The Causes of Battles

The emigration of all muslims and the Prophet from Makkah angered the kuffar. They had wanted to kill Muhammad but Allah saved him from their sinister designs. They could not see the small community of muslims living in peace elsewhere. They ambushed them and robbed or killed the isolated travellers. They teamed up with other kuffar communities around Madinah to perpetuate their ill treatment of the muslims. They even had the local clans of Bani Israil join them in their hostile plans, and make mischief against the muslims in Madinah and in the Jewish habitations near the city. The Makkans were furious because Muhammad asked them to worship Allah the one and only God, and taught them respect for life in general, and mutual love and tolerance amongst humans. The Prophet however did not sit back passively to take the insult from the enemy. He collected his believers and trained them to defend themselves, their families and their property against aggression or oppression. Although initially small in numbers and limited in resources, the Muslims were well armed with faith and confidence.

The Rules for the Battles

The Prophet had an exceptionally kind and gentle personality. He had shown his talent in peaceful settlement of quarrels amongst warring clans even before the proclamation of prophethood. The Prophet laid down 'Rules of Warfare' to be followed when it appeared to him that war was unavoidable to protect the Muslims and their families against the enemy's offence. These rules are listed below:

-Call upon Allah for help when you mount for a battle in His name

-Try and negotiate settlements with peace

-If you have to draw arms in war, do not resort to devious means in your battles and avoid the tactics of ambush

-Do not disfigure or dismember the fallen

-Do not kill or harm the old, the sick or the infirm, women and children

-Leave the monks and ascetics alone

-Do not cut or burn fruit trees

-Do not destroy cultivations or other vegetation

-Do not harm those who seek your protection. If they agree to pay the tythe for their safe conduct, accept it

-Allow the besieged to come out for peace or safe conduct

These rules made a revolutionary change in the old, brutal and ruthless methods of war amongst the Arabs of that time, and in the future. There was to be humanity and compassion even when the two parties had to come out in arms. It is a pity that the modern states and nations totally overlook these moral restraints in their conduct of war.

93

The Battles of the Prophet

Wars with the opposing forces of evil started from the first year of emigration of the muslims from Makkah. It would be difficult to describe each one of them in this booklet. The reader is referred to several other larger works that are available on the subject. Many of these battles were with the *kuffar* and Abu Sufyan bin Harb, the arch enemy of Islam. Others were with the mischievous Bani Israil in Madinah and at Khyber, in north east of Madinah. The major battles were Badr, Uhad, Khandaq, Hunayn and Khyber.

Treaty of Peace with the Kuffar

When the *kuffar* failed to weaken the Muslims in their faith, despite their tactics, they retracted into their stronghold in Makkah. By this time, the numbers of the Muslims had increased. They wanted to go for pilgrimage to the holy precinct of Ka'bah which is located in the heart of Makkah. When a large entourage of Muslims, accompanied by the Prophet approached Makkah, it made the *kuffar* nervous about the intentions of the Muslims. They intercepted and the Treaty of Hudaybiya was signed between the Muslims and the *kuffar* of Makkah. According to the terms of this treaty, Muslims would not enter the city that year. They performed their ritual sacrifices at their encampment, and returned to their homes. They were a little disappointed for not having been able to enter the holy precinct. The Prophet comforted them and said that they would all return to Makkah and perform their full rituals the following year.

The follwing year, the Muslims entered Makkah under the treaty. According to the agreement, the city was vacated by the kuffar who pitched their tents on the hills surrounding the holy precinct. They saw the muslims perform the rituals of Umra, all clad in white robes, quiet and sober in behaviour. There was no music or dancing or drinking or noise or screams. Their hearts were stirred by the discipline and organization of the Muslims.

The Conquest of Makkah

The mischief mongers among the kuffar caused breach in the peace treaty and killed some members of the Muslim alliance. Such conduct could not go unchallenged. The muslim community had to protect the rights of allies and their property. The leader of kuffar, the arch enemy of Islam, Abu Sufyan bin Harb went to Madinah to make repairs but he had to return to Makkah without forgiveness in this matter. Muhammad collected a large army of his faithfulls and marched on Makkah. The overwhelmed kuffar were unable to face this formidable force. When Abu Sufyan saw that he had no choice but to surrender, he accepted Islam and rushed home to tell others to do the same.

Muhammad declared total amnesty for all. The lives of all those who would gather under his banner, or keep inside their homes, or collect within the holy precinct of Ka'ba, or even those who would gather in the house of Abu Sufyan would be spared. They were to accept Allah as their supreme Lord, and Muhammad as His Messenger. This was a momentous day for the Muslims. They were back home to see their relatives and properties as free citizens. The mercy of the Prophet protected their former tormentors from revenge. The city of Makkah was declared as the city of Peace and sanctuary for all mankind.

Cleansing of Ka'ba from idols

The Prophet entered the gate of Ka'ba and joined Ali to break the idols which had for so long desecrated the House of Allah. The debris was quickly removed from the yard while the Muslims prepared for the first congregational prayer in the holy precict of Ka'ba. The numbers of the Muslims had swelled with the addition of the new converts. Bilal, the African, called out the *Azan* (the call for prayers) in his melodious style which brought tears in the eyes of the people. The events of past few years went rapidly through their minds and they thanked Allah for His mercy and benevolence.

Sura Barat

Whereas the Ka'ba had been cleansed, and the style of Hajj and Umra had been established by the Prophet himself, the kuffar from other districts were unaware of the recent changes. They would come to Makkah in the old style, singing and dancing, howling and screaming, exposing their bodies and carying idols and pagan offerings, unbefitting the piety restored to the sanctuary and the city of peace. As the sacred season of the year 9AH was approaching, Allah sent sura Barat to be announced to the pilgrims. It was to forbid the entry of all idolators in the sanctuary of Ka'ba. Abu Bakar was deputed to carry out this function. He was gone only a short distance when the

Prophet received a Command from Allah and in compliance with it, he instructed Ali to overtake Abu Bakar, take back the verses and himself announce these to the pilgrims at Makkah, on behalf of the Prophet. Abu Baker returned to Madinah with his entourage.

Mubahila with the Christians of Najran

In the same year, the message of Islam was conveyed to the Christians of Najran. They were invited to believe in the Oneness of Allah, give up the false belief in Trinity and the distorted notion that Jesus (Isa) was the Son of God. This was followed by long discussions and debates in Madinah, but the Christian bishops held fast to their beliefs. While this argument was in progress, the Prophet received a revelation : "...And he who disputes with thee concerning him after the truth had come to thee, say thou, come, let us call together our sons, and your sons, our women and your women, and our selves and your selves, then let us invoke and lay the curse of Allah on the liars." The Christian were informed and they accepted to meet the Prophet at an open place. On the appointed day and time, the Prophet took with him his daughter Fatima, her two sons Hassan and Hussain, and his cousin and son-in-law Ali.

When the Christian priests saw this small group marching towards the arena, they saw in them the signs of extra-ordinary nature. Filled with an awe, they agreed to pay tax and withdrew from the contest.

Missionaries of Muhammad

The people of Yaman requested the Prophet to send them some one who would teach them Islam. The Prophet initially sent Khalid bin Walid, who quickly became unpopular due to his hostile manners. The Prophet recalled him and sent Ali to Yaman. The people of Yaman became very fond of Ali as a teacher. They had also known him as the champion of Islam in many important battles. Ali demonstrated his compassion for the people, and his depth of knowledge of the Qur'an.

The Last Hajj

By the tenth year of al-Hijra Islam had reached throughout the Arabian peninsula, and Ka'ba had been cleansed of all vestiges of paganism. The strict orders of conduct for Hajj and Umra had already been laid by Allah through His revelation of Sura Barat. The Prophet decided to perform the ritual of Hajj along with his friends and followers. Ali who was in the south, hastened to join the Prophet on this auspicious occasion, to perform the first complete ritual of Hajj, led personally by the Prophet.

The faithful came, drones upon drones, from all directions to join the Prophet on this blessed occasion. The Prophet conducted the Hajj complete in ceremonies and delivered his famous sermon at Jabal-an-Noor.

The Last Revelations from Allah

It was at Khum-e-Ghadir, about half way to Madinah when Jibril brought the last revelation from Allah: "...O though, Apostle, proclaim what has been sent down to thee from thy Lord; and if though did not, it was as if though had not completed thy mission at all (and fear not), Allah will defend thee against men; verily Allah guideth not the unbelieving people."

The Prophet, on receiving the above Commandment immediately stopped the caravan and recalled the Muslims who had already departed in different directions. Standing on top of a raised platform, made in a make-shift manner, with the camel seats, the Prophet then announced to the people that he was to leave them soon, and they should follow the two things he was leaving behind, Allah's Book (al-Qur'an) and his Ahle Bait. Then he took Ali's hand in his hand and raised him, proclaiming, "Whomsoever I am the guardian, Ali too will be his guardian." Muslims gave their greetings and assurance to Ali. When this was happening, the Prophet received his last revelation and after that there was not to be any revelation: "...This day, we have perfected your religion and perfected you in my grace."

Death of the Prophet

Soon after his return from the last Hajj, the Prophet passed away after a short illness. His death was deeply felt by his family, friends and thousands of his followers. He was the last prophet of Allah, who left a legacy of his complete and superb personality, his excellent conduct, the Qur'an, his family, his companions and a rich body of traditions to guide mankind for all times.

The Achievements of Muhammed

In a short period of ten years after his emigration from Makkah, the power of arrogance and ignorance had been completely routed, idolatory had been totally wiped out, and the Message of Allah had spread throughout the Arabian peninsula. The Prophet himself had already sent letters to the rulers of the neigboring lands to quit paganism and called them to accept Islam and true monotheism. The teachings of Islam had started to spill over to lands beyond Arabia. The glory of the House of Allah, the sanctuary for mankind, had been re-established. The ritual of Hajj became sanctified and the rules for its proper conduct were established. The Arabs, who were divided into splintered group of clans and tribes were wrought into a nation, charged with spirit and purpose. Within only fifty years after the death of the Prophet, the Muslim rulers had conquered vast lands and peoples from east to west. Conquests of hearts and minds with Islamic idealogy followed these conquests. Today over one billion Muslims harken to the Message of Islam in many ethnic communities throughout the world.

The rights of the individual were secured and the rights of others in society were established. Women were given the dignity and respect as wives, daughters, mothers or sisters. Their rightful place in society was recognized and their right of inheritance was established. The Prophet had given his followers a code of conduct which was to govern the lives of all generations of Muslims in the future. They were true then and are true today. Muhammad was truly the greatest of all messengers of Allah who had completed His mission on earth, and had sealed prophesy for all times to come.

Observations on life and character of Prophet Muhammad

- When someone approached him, the Prophet always paid him his full attention

- He spoke softly, briefly but precisely and clearly. He avoided purposeless speech or discussion

- While being addressed, he did not interrupt the speaker

- He pointed with hands not with eyes

- He smiled on happy occasions and never reacted with laughter

- He was always the first to offer greetings

- While shaking hands, he avoided pulling his hand

- He walked on earth with humility, and with a down ward gaze

- He greeted children with affection and always spoke to them with kindness

- He treated the elderly with compassion and respect

- He kept the good people arround him and preached to the misguided with kindness

- In a meeting, he had no reserved place, and sat at the available place

- While seated on the floor, he did not stretch his legs

- While seated with visitors, he was not the first to leave. He waited until the visitors left

- His company was always pleasant and informative

- The tone of speech and discussions were always low in his company

- He helped any one and every one with whatever he had at the time

- If, for any reason he was unable to fulfil the needs of one seeking assistance, he spoke to him kindly and begged for his/her forgiveness for not being able to provide the service at that time

- When some one spoke to him with rudeness, he remained quiet

- He was not seen to speak or deal with any one with anger

- His sayings and deeds were always in concordance with the Qur'an and the Will of Allah

- He sat at the same level with others and ate the same food as those who served him

- He did most of his own house-hold or other personal chores

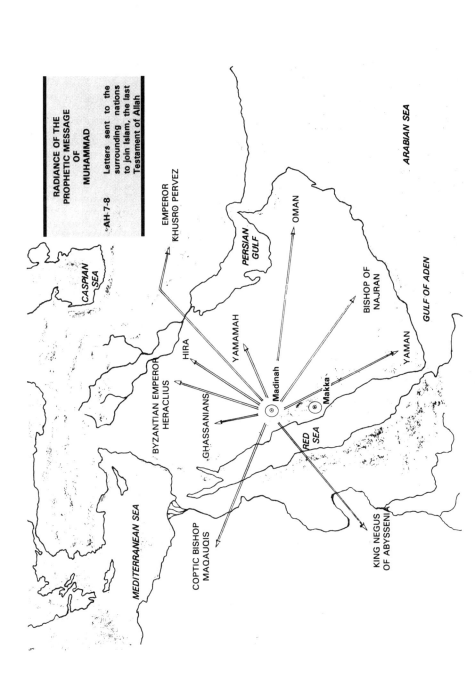

RADIANCE OF THE
PROPHETIC MESSAGE
OF
MUHAMMAD

•AH 7-8   Letters sent to the
surrounding nations
to join Islam, the last
Testament of Allah

EMPEROR
KHUSRO PERVEZ

CASPIAN
SEA

PERSIAN
GULF

OMAN

BISHOP OF
NAJRAN

ARABIAN SEA

GULF OF ADEN

YAMAN

YAMAMAH

HIRA

Madinah

Makka

RED
SEA

BYZANTIAN EMPEROR
HERACLIUS

GHASSANIANS

MEDITERRANEAN SEA

COPTIC BISHOP
MAQAUQIS

KING NEGUS
OF ABYSSENIA

- He mended his own attire, including his shoes

- He encouraged the owners not to cordon their fruit groves so that less fortunate may also enjoy the bounty of Allah

- He usually accepted invitation to have meals with friends and believers but told them that *sadaqah, khayrat and zakat* were *haram* for him

- He avoided colorful and decorative attire

- He treated his servants with kindness and never rebuked or punished them for error or mistake

- If a servant wanted his attention, Muhammad would get up and go to him before the servant could get to him

- He did not travel mounted while a companion was afoot

- He always kept his promise

- He slept little, and spent his time either in worship or serving others

- He had immense knowledge about all kinds of things and subjects although he never attended any formal school or other tutorship

- The Qur'an is the greatest miracle Allah bestowed on Muhammed for eternal benefit of all mankind.

SUGGESTED READINGS OF QUR'AN RELEVANT TO THE PROPHETS MENTIONED IN THIS BOOK

ADAM

I: 30-39; II: 34-36; III: 3; V: 27, 31; VII: 11-25, 189-190; XXV: 28-30; XVII: 61-62; XVIII: 50; XX: 120-128; XXXVIII: 71, 73; XLIX: 13.

IDRIS

XIX: 56-57; XXI: 85.

NUH

III: 33; VI: 85; VII: 59-64; X: 71-74; XI: 25-46; XIV: 9; XVII: 3; XXIII: 23-30; XXV: 37; XXVI: 105-122; XXIX: 14, 15; XXXVII: 75-83; LI: 46; LIII: 52; LIV: 9-16; LVII: 26; LXVI: 10; LXIX: 11; LXXI: 1-29.

HUD AND THE A'AD

VII: 65-72; XI: 50-60; XIV: 9; XXV: 38; XXVI: 123-140; XXIX: 38; XLI: 13-16; XLVI: 21-26; LI: 41-42; LIII: 50; LXIX: 4-8.

SALEH AND THE THAMUD

VII: 73-79; II: 61-68; XIV: 9; XV: 80, 84; XVII: 59; XXVI: 141-159; XXVII: 45, 53; XXIX: 38; XLI: 13-15, 17, 18; LI: 43, 45; LII: 51; LIV: 23, 31; LXIX: 4, 5; LXXXV: 18-20; XCI: 11-15.

IBRAHIM

II: 124-132, 135, 285, 260; III: 65-68, 95-97; IV: 35; VI: 75, 84, 85; IX: 114; XI: 69, 96; XII: 6; XIV: 35, 41; XV: 51,58; XVI: 120-122; XIX: 41, 50; XXI: 51, 53; XXII: 26-27; XVI: 69, 102; XXIX: 16-27, 31; XXXVII: 83, 102; XXXVIII: 45-47; XLIII: 26-28; LI: 24-32; LIII: 27; LV!I: 36; LX: 4-6; LXXXVII: 19.

LUT

VI: 87; VII: 80, 84; XI: 77, 83; XV: 57, 58; XXI: 71, 74-75; XXV: 40; XXVI: 160, 175; XXVII: 54-55; XXIX: 26, 28, 30, 33, 45; XXXVII: 33, 38; LI: 32, 37; LIII: 53; LIV: 33, 39; LXVI: 10.

ISMAIL

II: 125, 129, 133; VI: 87; XIX: 54-55; XXXVII: 101, 107; XXXVIII: 48.

ISHAQ

II: 123; VI: 85; XII: 6; XV: 53; XXI: 72-73; XXXVII: 112-113; XXXVIII: 45-47; LI: 28-30.

YA'QUB

II: 132; III: 93; VI: 85; XII: 4-101; XXI: 72-73; XXXVIII: 45-47; XL: 34.

YUSUF

XII: 4-101; XL: 34.

SHO'AYB

VII: 85, 93; XI: 84, 95; XV: 78, 79; XXVI: 176, 190; XXIX: 36-37.

MUSA AND HARUN

II: 40, 40-60, 63-66, 72-80, 83-98, 100-101, 108-109, 111, 113, 120-123, 134, 141, 145, 160, 174, 176, 211; III: 19-25, 54, 69, 80, 83, 99, 101, 110, 115, 181, 184, 188; IV: 44, 47, 49, 55, 123, 131, 153, 155, 60, 162, 164; V: 13-15, 18-26, 32, 59, 66, 68, 70, 76, 83; VI: 21, 55, 88, 91, 146, 155, 160; VII: 103, 156, 159, 171; VIII: 54; X: 75, 93; XI: 17, 96, 100, 110; XIII: 36; XIV: 5-8; XVI: 118, 124; XVII: 2-8, 101, 104; XIX: 51, 52; XX: 9-103; XXI: 48-49; XXIII: 45-49; XV: 35-36; XXVI: 10, 68; XXVII: 7-14; XXVIII: 30-46, 52, 55; XXIX: 39-40, 47; XXXII: 23-24; XXXIII: 26, 69; XXXVII: 113, 122; XL: 22-46, 53-54; XLI: 45; XLIII: 46, 56; XLIV: 17, 33; XLV: 16-17; XLVI: 12; LI: 38, 40; LIV: 41, 43; LVII: 26; LXI: 5; LXII: 5-8; LXIX: 9-10; LXXIII: 15-16; LXXIX: 15-26; LXXXV: 17-18; LXXXVII: 18-19; LXXXIX: 10-14.

YUSHA' BIN NUN

V: 23; XVIII: 60-65; LVI: 10.

SAMUEL

II: 247, 252.

DA'UD

II: 252; IV: 163; V: 77; VI: 85; XVII: 55; XXVII: 15-16; XXXIV: 10-11; XXXVIII: 17, 26, 30.

SULAYMAN

II: 102; IV: 163; VI: 87; XXI: 78, 82; XXVII: 15-42; XXXIV: XXXVIII: 30-40.

AYUB

VI: 85; XXI: 83-84; XXXVIII: 21-24.

ILYAS

VI:86,88; XXXVII: 123, 129.

ZULKIFL

XXI: 85; XXXVIII: 48.

AL-YASA'

VI: 87, 88; XXXVIII: 48.

YUNUS

IV: 163; VI: 87; X: 98; XXI: 87-88; XXXVI: 13, 21; XXXVII: 139, 148; LXVIII: 48-50.

UZAIR

II: 259; IX: 30.

LUQMAN

XXXI: 12-19.

ZAKARIYA

III: 37, 41; VI: 86; XIX: 1-15; XXI: 89.

YAHYA

III: 38-41; VI: 86; XIX: 5-15; XXI: 90; XXXVI: 13-41.

ISA

II: 87, 136, 253; III: 45, 62; IV: 157, 159, 163, 171-172; V: 18, 47, 72, 77, 110, 118; VI: 86; XIX: 19, 34; XXI: 90; XXII: 50; XLIII: 57, 64; LVII: 27; LXI: 6, 14.

II: 4, 89, 151; III: 143; IV: 61, 64-65, 69, 80, 82; V: 19; VI: 33, 191; VII: 156, 184; IX: 62; XVI: 82, 103; XVII: 1; XX: 1; XXI: 41, 107, 132; XXVIII: 46; XXX: 41; XXXIII: 6, 40; XXXVI: 1; XLI: 6; XLIII: 86; XLVII: 1, 2; XLVIII: 8, 29; LXI: 6; LXXII: 1, 19; LXXIII: 1-9; LXXXVII: 6-7; XCIII: 6; XCIV: 4.

AL-HUDA FOUNDATION, INC.

35 West Demarest Avenue, Englewood, NJ 07631

Phone : (201) 569-8123　　　　　　　　FAX : (201) 871-1927

BOOK SERVICE

Please send me .... copies of QUR'AN (Specify Translation)

☐ English Only　　　　☐ Englsih with Arabic

Price per copy (any translation) Soft Cover: $ 12.00　Hard Cover: $ 20.00

.... copies of PROPHETS OF ISLAM
by Syed Muhammad Hussain Shamsi

Price per copy　　　　　　Soft Cover Only: $ 7.00

☐　Payment enclosed (we pay shipping and handling on all pre-payment

☐　C.O.D.　　　　　　　(You pay shipping and handling)

☐　Terms available on bulk orders

A large selection of other popular books on Islam and Muslims is available. Please write to us about your interests or needs, and ask for our comprehensive catalog today.

NAME　　　　_____

ADDRESS:　_____

_____

Please fold and seal here, apply stamp, and mail it today!